After Adam

AFTER ADAM
The Books of Moses

Laurance Wieder

TO THE READER

After Adam is a *prosimetrum*, a story told in prose and verse. Mortality is its theme. Populated by rabbis, storytellers, mystics, poets, travelers and philosophers, the book belongs to the same small tribe as *The 1001 Nights,* Snorri Sturluson's *Heimskringla,* Dante's *Vita Nuova,* Sir Philip Sidney's *The Countess of Pembroke's Arcadia,* and Vladimir Nabokov's *Pale Fire.*

Each chapter in this Old Testament saga corresponds with a Sabbath portion of Moses' five books, as written in the *Tanakh,* the Hebrew Bible. I think of my synagogue—Congregation Beth Israel in Charlottesville, Virginia—and its traditional, lay-led *minyan* reading aloud from the Torah scroll every Saturday morning as Jewish Arcadians, gathering to recount the living history in tale and song.

To keep these fifty-four recitations as direct as possible, bible verses drawn from the chapter in question are not cited; footnotes identify cross-referenced biblical passages; and specific sources appear in the endnotes. Some of the psalms quoted here come from the *King James Version*; others, less familiar, are my own translations, first published in *Words to God's Music.*

As for the Hebrew Bible:

Everything seen in this world is found in the Book.
Some things found in the Book are not seen in this world.

—Laurance Wieder

UNDERSTOOD

She said: If only I could find the songbird's perch
By ear, if eyes could follow sound.
I said: They can. Look: that gray catbird
In the redbud turns the color of the leaves.
She: I see. But look away and, even if the bird remains,
The sight if not its song is lost.
Like reading from a Torah scroll:
Look up for just a moment and
You lose the place, and must fall silent
Until you find your place again.

TABLE OF CONTENTS

Genesis

IN THE BEGINNING
THE FIRST QUESTION, A STORY, ANOTHER QUESTION, AND A SONG
BERE'SHIT/בראשית—Genesis 1:1-6:8
In the beginning God created the heaven and the earth.

What did Adam know?

When creation began, God asked the angels:
"Shall we make man?"

They demurred: "Master of universes,
What is man, that you should think of him?"[a]

The One replied: "He will know more than you do."

Then God assembled all the animals, passed them before the angels, and asked: "What are these creatures?"

The angels could not say.

Next God created man (male and female), again assembled all the animals, and made them parade.

He asked the man: "What are these?"

The man replied: "Call this one 'horse;' this name 'lion;' this one, 'camel;' this one call 'ox;' this 'eagle;' this 'ass.'"

So man named all cattle, the fowl of the air, and every beast of the field.

God asked: "And you, what is your name?"

He answered: "'Adam.' I was fashioned out of earth [אֲדָמָה/adamah]."

God asked: "And what is my Name?"

Adam answered: "'[יהוה] LORD.'
You LORD over all Your works."

According to Rabbi Aḥa, God said:
"Yes, I am the Name,[b]
the One Adam called me, as do the angels."

---

a. Psalm 8:5
b. Isaiah 42:8

11

From that One's perspective, this world and the world-to-come were created all at once, like light and darkness, Eve and Adam, and what we know emerges like seed from the earth, or a scroll rolled out in time.

Judah Halevi's *Kuzari* is an extended dialogue between a rabbi and the eighth-century ruler of the Jewish kingdom of the Khazars. Deep in their discussion, the king wonders how he can understand the Name, which is not said aloud. "Can I grasp a matter I can't point to?"

The rabbi assures the Turkic convert that such was possible through prophecy or in a vision, but not by logical demonstration. "Philosophers deduce a Being which neither benefits nor injures, knows nothing of our prayers or disobedience, and so conclude that this world is as eternal as its Maker. None gives a proper name to God. Instead, philosophers assign some word to name the object of their speculation, convinced that reason made the World from nought.

"The first man never would have known the Name," the rabbi continued, "had the One not addressed, rewarded and punished him, and in sleep made separate Eve from his own rib. So Adam was convinced this presence, whom he named LORD, created all.

"The Tetragrammaton, the Name, is used only by Jews."[1]

The Maker said:
　　"I brought Adam into Eden.
　I gave him one command, but he transgressed.
　I spoke the sentence: 'Separated, banished.'
　I cried aloud: 'Where are you?
　　How alone?'"
God howled, if one dare speak that way, lamenting in his grief.

In one tradition, the human was created on Sabbath eve:
In the first hour, God made him in thought;
in the second hour, God consulted with the angels;
in the third, God gathered the dust;
in the fourth, God kneaded the dust;
in the fifth hour, God fashioned the parts;
in the sixth hour, God joined the parts;
in the seventh, God breathed into him;
in the eighth, God stood him on his feet;
in the ninth, God gave man one command;
in the tenth hour, Adam named the animals, and fell asleep, and dreamed and woke and knew his wife and disobeyed and named her Eve, because she was the mother of all living;
in the eleventh hour, God judged them as one;
in the twelfth hour, they were driven out.

Because the Sabbath intervened, Eve and Adam were expelled from Eden, not destroyed as God decreed.

At the close of Sabbath, Adam saw night creep up on him. He struck his face and cried out: "Woe! Is this that darkness where the serpent bruises me?"

God conducted Adam to two stones—one of thick darkness, the other of death's shadow—and taught him to strike two stones together, making sparks. Then Adam said:
"Blessed art Thou who created the light of the fire."[2]

The Sabbath rescued the first parents, but their first-born's knowledge of his own imperfection saved the first murderer from harsh judgment.

God decreed: "A fugitive and wanderer Cain shall be."

When Cain agreed, "My sin is greater than can be forgiven," half his punishment was canceled.

He left the Presence to wander east of Eden—only a wanderer, not a fugitive.

As Cain departed, Adam asked, "What was your sentence?"

His son answered, "I repented and was granted mercy."

Adam slapped his forehead, sighed, and said, "Too bad I did not know that."[3] And then recited a repentant's song:[a]

Thank you. I love
To sing at first light,
Pluck a gut string
In the watches of the night:
A little song, with rocks
And sea, and sky, without
Confusion of the parts.

Rocks sink. The sea is deep.
It holds the sky's dear
Face, the sun and moon
Also. Life started here.
Fools don't believe
This, think the waters
Tame and sounded,
Something with a name.

I heard music, foghorns
Over jetties, smelled
Sap from fresh-cut cedar

---

a. Psalm 92

Trees that grew straight
Up the mountain slopes
Of Lebanon. Let me grow
Old, let my sap run.

NOAH
OF HUMAN IMAGINATION, AND THE FRUITS OF EXPERIENCE

NOAH/נח—Genesis 6:9-11:32
These, the generations of Noah: Noah—
a just man upright in his time—
Noah walked with God.

I called out to the one who heard me say,
Save me from the plausible liars.
What can be said to a twister of truth, someone
Who preys upon trust, who mints coin from desire?
Bludgeon the bastards with bricks and bats, fire
Them, forbid them to sit on a bench in the sun?
No matter what I say, they contradict it. I say,
Peace, my soul wants peace. But they say, War.[a]

Noah's Flood and the Tower of Babel tell of the second creation and Fall. They account for the received world, imagined and made by man—God's image—from existing mud, after God made the heavens and the earth by saying, and from nothing.

Genesis recounts ten generations from Adam to Noah, and again, ten generations from Noah to Abraham, marking the temporal limit of Divine patience.

The Sages observed: When God hid his face from the generation of the Flood, he established the world from a single man, Noah.

Adam brought death into the world. But before the Flood, people never died young, nor suffered cold and fever. They only needed to plant one crop to feed themselves for forty years. They could travel from one end of the world to the other in no time flat, uprooting trees while they walked. They took no more

---

a. Psalm 120

16

notice of a lion's or leopard's bite than that of a flea. As for the weather, it was always mild, like the time between the Festival of Unleavened Bread and the Festival of Weeks.

One of the great men of a later time—some say Rabbi Samuel son of Naḥmani—had a headache, and lamented, "This is what the generation of the Flood did for us."

As Noah stepped out from the ark, the lion clawed his genitals. So later, when that man (who was born circumcised) sported with a woman, his seed scattered, and he was humiliated.

According to the Rabbis, after Noah planted a vineyard and drank too much wine, his middle son Ham entered the paternal tent, saw his father's nakedness and castrated him.

In return, Noah cursed Ham, saying "Your sons will serve his brothers and, because you have kept me from pleasure in the dark, as a servant desires the shadow,[a] your seed will be dark and ugly."

Rabbi Ḥiyya added, "Belowdecks in the ark, Ham coupled with a dog."

"That is," Rabbi Levi explained, "Ham tried stamping his own coin, to make a creature in his own image. And this in God's house."[4]

"The imagination of the heart of man is evil from his youth."

In Psalm 92, when David sings "I will give thanks to the LORD with my whole heart," he means, "with both my Inclination-to-Good and my Inclination-to-Evil, so that my heart should not be in conflict."

A midrash cautions that a man who walks with a companion, after a time becomes his friend. But the evil

---

a. Job 7:2

imagination is inborn, and grows up with a person. Given the opportunity, it will overwhelm him. You have no greater enemy.[5]

In another legend, Noah saved the coats of skins that God made for Adam and Eve to clothe their nakedness. After the Flood abated, Ham took Adam's coat and gave it as an inheritance to his grandson, Nimrod. When Nimrod put on Adam's coat, every animal, beast and bird lay down before him. The Assyrians thought this was an homage to Nimrod's own power, so they made him king.

"And the whole earth was of one language, and of one speech."

The people of the plain said, "Once every thousand, six-hundred fifty-six years (the span from Adam to Noah) the firmament totters, as it did in the Flood. Let's be provident and raise supports for heaven here in Shinar, in the east. Come, let us build a City and a Tower and a Name."

Lacking stones to build their city, Nimrod's masons baked bricks. Workers carried hods up a ramp on the east, and went down on a ramp to the west.

Work went so smoothly that a man laying one brick found two bricks had been laid; another spreading mortar over one course found two courses had been set.

The tower rose seven miles high. When a laborer fell from the height, they paid no heed. But if a brick dropped they sat down and wept, "Woe is us. When will another come in its stead?"

Nimrod told his people, "Why settle for life in the lower world, while God takes the upper for himself? Let us ascend to heaven and beat him with axes."

They formed into three groups.

The first one said, "Let us go up and dwell there." From there, God scattered them.

The second group waged war on heaven, and were transformed into monkeys, spirits and demons.

The third contingent said, "Let us raise idols on high."

Abraham the son of Terah watched them construct the city and tower, and cursed the builders, praying:

"Destroy, O LORD, divide their tongues."[a]

God swore: "You say 'Let us come up.'

I say, 'Let us come down, and there confuse their language.'"[6]

The Hebrew verb חָלַל/ḥalal [to pollute, defile, profane] also means "to begin." It first appears in Genesis 4:26,

when men began to call upon the name of the LORD;

again in chapter 6, when men began to multiply on the face of the earth;

after the Flood, when Noah began to be an husbandman;

and when God said of Nimrod's kingdom:

"Behold: one people, and they all have one language,

and this they begin to do."

Before the birth of David, when God told the child Samuel what He would perform against Eli's sons' unrestrained evil, He offered the prophet this rare bit of explication:

"When I begin, I also make an end."[b]

"And the LORD came down to see what the sons of man had built."

Nimrod's nation could have imagined and made another heaven, on the earth. Instead, they raised a city and the Tower.

a. Psalm 55:9
b. 1 Samuel 3:12

In David's prayer—
"Do not kill them, so my people won't forget. LORD,
>   Scatter them, and bring them down
>   For their foul mouths and loose lips.
>   Take them in their pride.
>   Curse their lying speech"—[a]
"they" are the builders of the Tower.

Judah bar Naḥmani observed, "This generation following the Flood, you'd think they'd profit from the experience of the one preceding, no?"[7]

As for the tower they built, a third was burned, a third was swallowed up, and a third remained. From atop that ruin, the palms of Jericho look like grasshoppers.[8]

The Assyrians called בָּבֶל/bavel [Babel or Babylon] *Bab-ilu*, gate of god.

"Therefore is the name of the city called Babel; because the LORD did there confound the language of all the earth: and from thence did the LORD scatter them abroad upon the face of all the earth."

Rashi compared the annihilation of the Flood to the dispersion of mankind: "Noah's generation did not stretch forth their hands against God, but there was strife among them, and they were drowned; Nimrod's kingdom waged war against God, but the people conducted themselves with love and friendship toward each other, in one language and one speech.

"And so they lived.

"Violence is hated, and great is peace."

---

a. Psalm 59:11-12

Rabbi Ḥiyya adds, "All depends upon the word of mouth. As soon as their speech was scrambled, God scattered them. But in a time to come, the LORD will purify the many languages into one, so all may call upon the Name and serve him."[a]

And on that day, Zechariah[b] wrote,

"The LORD will be one and his name, One."[9]

---

a. Zephaniah 3:9
b. Zechariah 14:9

GO FOR YOURSELF
GOD'S PROMISE TO ABRAHAM; CUTTING-OFF, AND ADDING-ON

LEKH LEKHA/לך־לך—Genesis 12:1-17:27
Now the LORD said to Abram: You,
go for yourself from your country,
from your kindred and from your fathers house,
to the land that I will show you.

Abram's father Terah made idols in Ur of the Chaldees,
Nimrod's kingdom in the plain of Shinar.

A midrash records that at Abram's birth, a star rose in the
east and swallowed four stars in the four corners of heaven.
Nimrod's wizards understood the portent referred to Terah's
son, and sought to kill him.

The boy hid in a cave for three, or some say thirteen, years.
When he emerged from the darkness, Abram looked at the stars,
the moon, the rising sun and wondered to himself,

"Who made all this and me?"
and answered in the holy language:

"O Creator, LORD of Hosts,
blessed the man who trusts in you."[a]

Rabbi Simeon ben Yoḥai speculated that, since Terah did not
teach him and Abram had no master to instruct him, the holy
One filled Abraham with Torah and wisdom. "No," Rabbi Levi
said, "Abraham learned Torah by himself."[10]

Simeon's son Eleazar looked to the text: God's command
"Go for yourself" means "Refine yourself—do not stay here
among idolators."[11]

In another legend, Abram's younger brothers insisted that
since Abram would not sell their idols, he should be made a

---

a. Psalm 84:12

priest. Terah instructed his first-born to set food and drink before the statues, and wait for them to accept the offerings.

A woman brought Abram a bowl of fine flour for the gods. It sat untouched. Abram broke the small gods with a stick, put the stick in the hand of the biggest idol, and waited.

His father asked, "What happened to the gods?"

Abram told him, "A woman brought an offering, and the gods argued over who should eat first. The biggest one rose up and smashed the others."

Terah snapped, "Don't joke. These gods cannot do anything."

Abram replied, "So you say. Let your ears hear what your mouth tells you."[12]

There is no before or after in the Torah.

From God's perspective, all creation is gathered in a single flash, outside time. This past-present-future spectacle resembles the dream world, where something other than temporal sequence or reason or cause-and-effect orders what unfolds. So, when it tells the events of Abraham's life—from God's command to the seventy-year-old Abram to "Go" through Abraham's circumcision at age ninety-nine—Scripture may appear disordered.

According to the rabbinic chronology *Seder Olam*, after God first spoke to him in Haran, Abram went to Canaan, returned to Haran, then five years later left again for Canaan. On that second journey, as told in Genesis 14, the patriarch passed through Egypt, settled in Hebron and, that same year, battled the four kings who conquered Sodom and Gomorrah.

One who escaped the fall of Sodom brought news of Lot's capture to "Abram the Hebrew"—the first occurrence of the word Hebrew [עִבְרִי/ivri] in the Books of Moses. God called Abram "the Hebrew," Rabbi Tanḥuma[13] explained, because while idol worshippers arrayed on one side of a valley, Abram עָבַר/avar [passed over] and stood alone against the nations.

After these things, the word of the LORD came to Abram in a vision, saying: "Fear not."

The rabbis divide this prophetic interlude—between Abram's military triumph and Ishmael's birth one chapter later—into two. The spoken vision of the first six verses, where God promises the still childless Abram that his seed will be innumerable as stars, follows the just-recounted events.

The rest of the chapter, which opens with a blood ritual and closes with the covenant granting Canaan to Abram's numberless seed, they assign to a time five years and three chapters previous when the LORD said, "Go you forth."

Wherever located, Abram's vision, dream sacrifice and God's covenant speak to his lifelong question:

"LORD, what can you give me, seeing I go childless?"

God promises Abram that he will have a son from Sarai, and his heirs will inherit the land of Canaan.

When Abram wondered: "How shall I know I will inherit it?" God directed Abram to sacrifice a heifer, a she goat, a ram, a turtle dove and a young pigeon.

Abram cut the herd animals in half, but left the dove and pigeon whole. Carrion birds circled the carcasses, but Abram drove them off as the sun set and

A deep sleep fell upon Abram and, lo,
an horror of darkness fell upon him, and

behold! a smoking furnace, and a burning lamp
passed between those pieces of the sacrifice.

That same day the LORD cut a covenant with Abram, saying, "Unto thy seed I have given this land."

Rashi reads the promise to Abram, "I will make you a great nation" in its plainest sense: "I will add a letter to your name: Abram will become Abraham."

Rabbi Berekiah interprets "I will make you" to mean "I will create you anew, and you will be fruitful and multiply."[14]

Rav Kahana added that only two men in all Israel—Abraham and Isaiah—fit the Psalmist's description:

"You have loved right and hated wickedness;
and so your God has anointed you above your fellows
with the oil of gladness, to bring comfort and healing."[a]

Over the ten generations from Noah to Abraham, God spoke to no one. But God made a new beginning when he said to Abram: "Fear not."

Thirteen years later, the LORD appeared to Abram and said to him: "I am God Almighty: Walk before Me and be perfect," which meant, "be circumcised."

Saadia Gaon wondered how it could be that a man's body in its complete natural state is imperfect but, when something is cut off, it becomes perfect? He suggests that the Creator made one part of the body with a redundancy. Remove the redundant and what remains is perfection.

A midrash on Psalm 112 insists that Abraham kept the commandments with delight. When God saidl, "He that is born in thy house...must needs be circumcised," Abraham circumcised himself on the same day.

The patriarch did ask God, "If circumcision is so precious, why was it not given to Adam?"

---

a. Psalm 45:8

The holy One answered, "Let it be enough for you that you and I are in the world."

Abraham rejoined, "Before I circumcised myself, men came and joined me in my new faith. Will they come now?"

God closed, "Abraham, it is enough that I am your God—enough not just for you, but for My world."[15]

When one letter was added to Abram's name he became Abraham, as Sarai became Sarah.

When something was subtracted, he could beget, and she could bear, though both were very old.

HE APPEARED
DISTINGUISHES BETWEEN THEORY AND PRACTICE

VA-YERA'/וירא—Genesis 18:1-22:24
The LORD appeared to him in the plains of Mamre:
and he sat in the tent door in the heat of the day.

And the LORD said:
"Shall I hide from Abraham that thing which I will do?"

The Rabbis teach: One who translates Torah is forbidden to look into the scroll and translate, lest people think that the translation is written in the Torah itself.

Also, when reading Torah aloud, the reader's eyes may not wander from the scroll, because the Law was given only in written form.

Yehudah ben Pazi explained: "God said to Moses, 'Write these words for yourself,' which shows the Torah was given in writing. He finished saying, 'By these words I have made a covenant with you,'[a] which means their understanding was by word-of-mouth."[16]

Maimonides admonished theoretical speculators, who fancy they can understand Scripture by leafing through it as one might turn the pages of a history or a book of poetry, that "Things are not as you thought. The intellect, which God made the ultimate human perfection, lived in Adam before he disobeyed. It was this image of himself in man that the Creator spoke to, and commanded."[b]

When the LORD appeared to him in the plains of Mamre, Abraham saw with his mind, not with the eye, since the eye can only apprehend a body.

a. Exodus 34:27
b. Genesis 2:16

Messengers take different forms in prophetic vision. To some prophets they appear as human individuals, to others, angels. The Sages note that Abraham's prophetic power was great, and the angels appeared before him as three men; to Lot, who was weak, the messengers appeared as angels.[17]

According to another commentary, three faculties are found in man: the rational, the thoughtful, and the imaginative.

The noblest faculty, the rational, is named Raphael.

The thoughtful, known as Michael, rescued Lot.

Gabriel is the imagination, through which Sodom was destroyed.[18]

Abraham approached one messenger and said,

"Will you destroy the righteous with the wicked?"

Rabbi Levi observed that, when Job asked God the same question, Job concluded that, for himself,

"All is one; He destroys the upright and the wicked."[a]

But Abraham answered for God within himself—

"That would be far from You"—

and rested his defense with a question:

"Shall not the Judge of all the earth do right?"

The conventional gloss on human trials found in the Torah treats them as tests of the faith or obedience of an individual or nation. But the case is not that easy. Moses calls the One "A God of faithfulness and without iniquity."[b] And some sages maintain that there is no death without sin and no suffering without transgression.[19] These simultaneous assumptions cinch the knot at the heart of the Binding of Isaac, where afterward Abraham was told, "Now I know that you fear God."

a. Job 9:22
b. Deuteronomy 32:4

In the *Guide of the Perplexed*, the patriarchal story embodies two fundamental principles:

First, it demonstrates the limit of love for God, and shows how far one must go for fear of Him. Abraham hastened to slaughter Isaac not because he was afraid that God would kill him or make him poor, but because he loved and feared God without hope of reward or fear of punishment.

Second, the binding teaches that prophets regard what God reveals to them as undoubted truth. Thus Abraham, the first prophet, did not hesitate to sacrifice Isaac, whom he loved, even though word came to him in a night vision. Had the prophetic dream been obscure or inspired doubt, would a father obey such an unnatural command? And, Maimonides concludes, the Omniscient does not need to test a thing in order to discover what He did not know.[20]

The trial reveals how difficult it is to love, and fear, and believe.

Judah Halevi, who perished on his way to Jerusalem, held that God tempted Abraham in order to render theoretical obedience practical, and let it be the cause of the patriarch's prosperity. And so God said,

"Because you have done this thing... I will bless you."[21]

On the day Isaac was weaned, Abraham made a great feast.

That same day, the angel Samael said to God,
"Master of the Universe,

You gave this hundred-year-old man a son,
yet he has not offered you so much as a single pigeon."

God answered, "Abraham feasts to honor Isaac.
Were I to say 'Sacrifice your son to me,' he would."[22]

God said to Abraham, "Take your son Isaac and get into the land of fear, Moriah, and offer him there as a burnt offering, on a mountain I will tell you of."

Abraham woke early in the morning, saddled his ass, took two of his young men, and Isaac his son, split wood for the burnt offering, rose up, and went to the place God told him.

On the way, Samael disguised as an old man met him and asked, "Where are you going?"

Abraham answered, "To pray."

The Satan queried, "Does prayer require wood, fire, and a knife?"

He countered, "If I pray for several days, I will need to slaughter, cook and eat an animal."

The Adversary barked, "I was present when God ordered 'Take your son.' Would you destroy the child of your old age, and think to beg another? This is Satan's work."

Abraham replied, "God commanded me, not you. Away!"

Next Samael drew near to Isaac, in the shape of a young man, and asked, "Where are you going?"

Isaac said, "To study how to call on my Creator."

Satan mocked, "You plan to learn this dead, or alive?"

Isaac vollied, "What can the dead know?"

The Adversary cried, "Unlucky son of an unhappy mother. How many years she hoped until she bore you, and now this mad old man will kill you on an altar."

Said Isaac, "Even so," and turning to his father asked, "Did you catch that?"

On the third day, Moriah came in view.

Again Satan appeared before Abraham, and proclaimed: "A message reached me from on high; a lamb, not Isaac, will be sacrificed."

Abraham growled, "Liar." Abraham took the wood, the fire, and the knife, and father and son went up together.

Then Isaac spoke to Abraham his father, "Behold the fire and the wood: but where is the lamb for a burnt offering?"

The Zohar[23] comments that, when he answered "God will provide Himself the sheep my son," Abraham was Isaac's adversary. He was really telling Isaac:

"God will provide for Himself when He needs to.

"But for now: my son, not a sheep."

And they walked on together.

When Abraham drew the blade to Isaac's throat, Satan blocked his hand, and the knife dropped.

As the father reached to pick it up, a voice said, "Abraham, Abraham. Raise not your hand against the boy."

Abraham asked, "Says who?"

The voice replied, "An angel."

Abraham shot back, "When God commanded, 'Take your only son,' He spoke himself.

"If he wants me to stop, let him say so."

Then God called: "Abraham!"

who heard, and answered, "Here am I."[24]

Rabbi Simeon the son of Yoḥai taught his son Eleazar: "Love upsets the natural order, and hate upsets the natural order.[25]

"Isaac was thirty-seven, and Abraham was an old man. Had Isaac kicked with one foot, Abraham could not have withstood him. Yet he honored his father, and allowed himself to be bound for sacrifice because the old one willed it."[26]

In another legend, when told to stay his hand, Abraham retorted, "God plays it both ways?

"Yesterday you said, 'Through Isaac shall your seed be called.'

"Then you turned about and told me, 'Take your son.'

"And now you bid me, 'Lay no hand upon him.'"

God answered, "Abraham, when I commanded 'Take your son,' did I say 'Slaughter him?'

"No. I said 'Take him up.'

"You have taken him up.

"Now take him down."[27]

SARAH'S LIFE
A CHAPTER OF MOTHERS, AND WIVES, AND OLD AGE
ḤAYYEI SARAH/חיי שרה—Genesis 23:1-25:18
Sarah was one hundred and twenty-seven years old:
these were the years of Sarah's life.

Before Abraham there was no old age. Consequently, a person who wished to speak with Abraham might mistakenly address Isaac, or someone wanting to engage Isaac might approach Abraham. So Abraham prayed:
"Master of the universe, enough confusion.
"Make visible the difference between young and old."
God answered, "I begin with you."
Abraham went to bed.
When he arose next morning, the patriarch was old, his beard and hair turned white.
He said, "This white hair is a mark of age? I do not like it."
God disagreed: "The hoary head is glory's crown."[a] [28]

After Isaac's birth, Sarah endured for thirty-seven years. The moment Abraham bound Isaac for sacrifice on Mount Moriah, she died. Those years, according to Rabbi Ḥiyya, were Sarah's true life.

While Abraham made his way back to Hebron, Satan accosted Sarah in the guise of an old man, asking "Have you heard how Abraham took Isaac up to the altar for a burnt offering and...?"

Sarah keened three long wails then three short shrieks—like the notes blown on the ram's horn at New Year—and her soul fled.

Abraham returned to Mamre from Mount Moriah and

---

a. Proverbs 16:31

buried Sarah, who died of grief. That, Rabbi Yose explains, is why the binding of Isaac appears close to the chapter, "Sarah's Life."

The *Book of Splendor* states that there was no other woman like Sarah: verses enumerate her days and years, and record both her existence in the world and the precise place where she was buried—Kiriath Arba.

According to tradition, before the holy One let Sarah's sun set, He made Rebekah's sun rise:[29]

When Sarah died, Rebekah was born.

The scholarly companions of the Zohar established that two never-before-yoked milk cows lowed a new song as they carted the ark from the land of the Philistines back to Israel.[a]

Yoḥanan said, "A calf without blemish, Rebekah returned. The cows sang, but which song?"

Simeon son of Yoḥai answered, "The orphaned psalm with no author, which starts:

'Sing a new song to the old sky, the new moon
A sickle for harvesting all we remember.'"[b]

Rabbi Eliezer's chapter "On Lovingkindness" marvels that the journey from Kiriath Arba to Haran took seventeen days, yet in three hours Abraham's servant Eliezer arrived at the fountain in Mesopotamia. Once there, Rebekah, a king's daughter who all her life had never gone to fetch water went out and drew water from the well. And the girl, who did not know this man, or any man, agreed to marry Isaac.

Rabbi Aha deemed the ordinary conversations of servants in the Patriarchs' household more important than the Torah

a. 1Samuel 6:12
b. Psalm 98

given to their descendants. Thus, Eliezer's mission fills several columns of text with mundane details like room and board, straw and fodder for camels, and provisions for his entourage. The steward's words are both reported and repeated. Even the washing of Abraham's servants' feet appears in the record.[30]

Riding camels, Abraham's servant left Haran at noon with Rebekah and Deborah her nurse. Again the journey was shortened, and in three hours they arrived at Hebron, at Kiriath Arba.

Isaac had gone out to meditate in the field toward evening, the time of afternoon prayer, covered with a blue shawl. When Rebekah arrived, she saw Isaac, and asked Eliezer,

"What man is this, whose prayer shawl appears like the cloak, the glory and majesty of God?"[a]

To Rabbi Hezekiah's eye, that blue appears to be the color of the sea, which waves like grass,

tall grass like trees that vault the canopy, the sky. There dawn appears like the rainbow,

bright beams from the cloud on the day of rain— as Ezekiel[b] said—'like the brightness that surrounds the appearance of the likeness of the LORD.'[31]

Isaac prayed:
I say the thing out loud
And to the LORD.

I bow down, I complain
About my troubles:
All, all alone in danger,
Grown a stranger

a. Psalm 104:1
b. Ezekiel 1:28

To ones who knew me once.
An orphaned soul,
    I raise my voice to you:
O LORD, my help
And place among the living,
    Hear me.[a]
Then Isaac brought Rebekah into the tent of Sarah his mother, and took her, and loved her, and was comforted.

Kiriath Arba, the City of Four, where Abraham purchased the cave of Machpelah, in Mamre, is the same place as Hebron in Canaan. "Four" refers to the men buried there, Adam, Abraham, Isaac, and Jacob, along with four Matriarchs: Eve, Sarah, Rebekah, and Leah.

Rabbi Banaah used to mark burial sites in Hebron, so that people would not stumble over one and become unclean.

One day, he came upon the cave of Machpelah. Abraham's servant Eliezer stood outside the entrance to Abraham's crypt. When Banaah asked what Abraham was doing, Eliezer replied, "He sleeps in Sarah's arms, and she gazes at his head."

Banaah asked Eliezer to inform the patriarch that he stood without, and wanted to come in.

Abraham said, "Let him enter."

The rabbi went in, measured the cave, and came out again.

Adam's burial chamber was right next to Abraham and Sarah's.

As Banaah moved to enter, a heavenly voice said:
"You have seen Abraham, the image of my likeness Adam. Adam, made in my own image, you may not look at."

---

a. Psalm 142

"But I need to mark the limits of the cave," Banaah protested.

The voice informed him: "The outer chamber where the Fathers and Mothers are buried is the same size as the inner chamber of Adam and Eve."

Rabbi Banaah reported later, "I saw Adam's heels, and they looked like a pair of suns."[32]

GENERATIONS
OF CHILDREN, BIRTHRIGHT, AND WHERE BLESSINGS BEGIN AND END

TOLEDOT/תולדת—Genesis 25:19-28:9
These are the generations of Isaac, Abrahams son:
Abraham begat Isaac.

The Patriarchs only died because each one requested death.
Abraham told God, "I speak, who am but dust and ashes."[a]
Isaac said to his son, "My soul may bless before I die."
And Jacob greeted Joseph, "Now let me die, since I have
seen your face, because you live."[b]
God said, "Let them make way for others:
Abraham for Isaac, Isaac for Jacob, Jacob for Israel."[33]

While they grappled in Rebekah's womb, Jacob proposed to
Esau, "My brother, our father Isaac has two sons, even as he
possesses two worlds—this one of eating and drinking and
business and marriage and begetting children, as well as the
world to come.

"Choose one, and I will take the other."

Esau replied, "The living die. You think the dead will live
again? Give me this world. You get the world to come."

Esau became a hunter, but Jacob was a plain man of the
tents. One day, as Jacob stewed lentils, Esau returned famished
from the field.

Esau asked, "What is this pottage?"

In one legend Jacob answered, "Our grandfather Abraham
is dead. This is a pot of mourning. See, just like a mourner a
lentil has no mouth and can not speak for sadness.

"Then again, lentil soup is served at banquets, and so gives

---

a. Genesis 18:27
b. Genesis 46:30

joy, just like a birthright."[34]

Esau demanded, "Feed me."

Jacob countered, "Have a taste for bread and lentils? Sell me your birthright."

Esau opened wide and ordered, "Shovel in that red, red pottage. Another bowlful and you can have my birthright."

The rabbis commented: Esau was red, his food red, his land red, his red warriors wore red garments, and his Avenger will come from Edom clad in red apparel splashed with blood.[a]

No sooner had Esau sold the birthright, then he sought to kill his brother.

All the good Isaac enjoyed in this life he owed to Abraham. But Isaac will ransom Abraham's descendants on the day of judgment.

God will say to Abraham, "Your children have sinned."

Abraham will reply, "Go. Wipe them out, and sanctify your Name."

God will then turn to Jacob, who will give the same answer.

Next, God will accuse Isaac, "Your children have sinned."

Isaac will parry, "Creator of the world, my children?

"When they stood before Sinai, You called them 'My first-born.' But if they are mine, not yours, it's no great thing to save them:

"By your own reckoning, children are not responsible until the age of twenty. Of the fifty years remaining of the allotted seventy, half the time is spent asleep, and half of that remainder's occupied by prayer, eating, and attending to needs. So only twelve and one-half wayward years need be redeemed.

---

a. Isaiah 63:1-3

"If that's still too much for you, take half, and put the other half on me."[35]

Another story: When Abraham bound Isaac for sacrifice, the angels of peace wept bitterly. Their tears dropped into Isaac's eyes and left a mark so that, when he grew old, his eyes were dim from seeing.

Isaac's blindness made it possible for Jacob to disguise himself in goatskins and pass for Esau, to get his blessing.

As Rabbi Eleazar tells it, their father said to Jacob, "Come near so I can feel you. Are you really my son Esau?"

Jacob replied, "I am," and feared he would be found out.

But Isaac from his dark place said:

"The voice Jacob's voice, but the hand the hand of Esau."

When Isaac did not know him, and blessed him, Jacob sang a Song of Ascents which begins:

"I called out to the One, who heard me say

Save me from the plausible liars."

Rabbi Eliezer observed that the first blessings Isaac gave to Jacob—the dew of heaven and the fatness of the earth, and plenty of corn and wine—concern the here and now. The final blessings—that people serve you and that nations and your brothers bow down to you, that all who curse you be cursed, and all who bless you be blessed—address the foundation of this world and of the world to come.

According to Rabbi Phinehas, when Israel, who cannot be numbered like the stars say "Hear, O Israel," the angels fall silent and drop their wings. Then, like God answering Job from the whirlwind, the morning stars sing together, and all the sons of heaven shout for joy.[a]

---

a. Job 38:7

To his own blessing, Isaac added the promise God gave Abraham, "To you and to your seed, to inherit the land where you are a stranger."

Jacob was yet scarce gone out from the presence of Isaac his father when Esau came in, and Isaac trembled very exceedingly. Esau entered from the daylight, and did not see Jacob kneeling in the dark. But Jacob saw Esau, and hid behind the door.

When Esau came in, Jacob slipped out.

Rabbi Yoḥanan asked, "When a man has two sons, and one goes out while the other goes in, does he tremble? However, when Esau entered his father's house, Hell came with him, and the walls began to seethe."[36]

Esau called, "Let my father arise and eat of his son's venison."

Isaac knew Esau's voice and asked: "Who then has taken and brought me venison? And I have eaten all before you came."

Esau asked, "What did Jacob actually give you to eat?"

Isaac replied, "I do not know, but it tasted of bread, of meat, of fish, the taste of locusts and the savor of all the fine things in this world."

At the mention of meat, Esau wept, "For that plate of lentils which he sold me, my brother took my birthright; how much more then for the meat he has given you."

When he heard Esau had sold Jacob the birthright, Isaac responded:

"Rightly did I bless him; and he shall be blessed."

Rav Kahana teaches that, if the reader standing before the ark makes a mistake, a new reader must take his place, and begin again at the blessing where the first one halted.[37]

Such was the practice of the Patriarchs: each began his blessing where his father before him ended.

So Abraham blessed Isaac:

"All that he had Abraham gave unto Isaac."

When Isaac blessed Jacob, he started where Abraham stopped, at "Therefore God give," and ended with:

"And Isaac called Jacob, and blessed him."

To bless the Tribes, Jacob called his sons, and finished with

"This, the blessing."[a]

When Moses stood before Israel for the last time, he opened where Jacob concluded, at

"This, the blessing."[b]

---

a. Genesis 49:28
b. Deuteronomy 33:1

HE LEFT
THE ANATOMY OF KISSES

VA-YETSE'/ויצא—Genesis 28:10-32:3
Jacob left Beer–sheba, and went toward Haran....
And Jacob kissed Rachel, and lifted up his voice, and wept.

Rabbinic tradition regards all kisses as frivolous, except for three:

the kiss of homage, as when Samuel poured oil over David's head, and kissed him, and said that the LORD anointed David captain over the inheritance of Israel;[a]

the kiss after long separation, such as Aaron's when he went into the Wilderness, met Moses at the mountain of God, and kissed him;[b]

and the kiss of parting like Orpah gave her mother-in-law.[c]

To these, Rabbi Tanḥuma adds the kiss of kinship, as when Jacob kissed Rachel at the well.

The verb נָשַׁק/nashaq [to kiss] is not common in Torah. This doesn't mean that no one kissed from the sixth day in Eden until that first recorded kiss, when dim-sighted Isaac told the disguised Jacob to "Come near now, and kiss me, my son." Rather, it suggests that the unrecorded kisses of before and aftertimes partake of lightness and the moment, are akin to play and laughter, as celebrated in Solomon's Song:

Let him kiss me with the kisses of his mouth:
for thy love is better than wine.

Like knowledge of good and evil, the first kiss was stolen. Jacob came near Isaac and he kissed him. More, when Isaac

a. 1Samuel 16:13
b. Exodus 4:27
c. Ruth 1:14

kissed his son, he also smelled the smell of his son's raiment, and blessed him. This "smell" derives from רוּחַ/ruaḥ—the wind-spirit-breath of creation.

In both the Hebrew and the English, it's not clear who kisses whom. Perhaps this kiss went both ways between father and son—foreshadowing Jacob's dream of angels ascending and descending a ladder between earth and heaven: between one who did not know whom he was kissing, and one who knew the other did not know.

Laban kissed Jacob in greeting, and at parting. When his nephew arrived in Padan-aram, Laban met, embraced and kissed him, and brought him to his house. Twenty years later, when Jacob stole away from his father-in-law to return to Canaan with what would be the seed and substance of Israel, Laban pursued Jacob, he said, in order to kiss his daughters and (grand)sons goodbye. The two made a covenant of peace between their houses. Then Laban rose up, kissed his sons and daughters, blessed them, and departed.

Esau ran to meet his returning brother, and embraced him, and fell on his neck, and kissed him: and they wept.

After Joseph revealed himself to Benjamin and his brothers, he kissed them all, and wept. When the brothers carried their father Israel down to Egypt, the old, blind patriarch brought Joseph, Manasseh and Ephraim near to him, and he kissed them and embraced them. At Jacob's death, Joseph fell upon his fathers face, and wept upon him, and kissed him.

On the other hand, Pharaoh's decree that all his people should kiss (meaning yield to) Joseph's mouth is, like the idolators who kiss calves in Hosea 13:2, frivolous.

The last kiss in the Torah belongs to Moses, who went out

Genesis

to meet his father-in-law, and did obeisance, and kissed him.[a]
More prophets tell of kisses: David and Jonathan kissed
and wept with one another; returning to Jerusalem, David
crossed back over Jordan, and kissed Barzillai, and blessed
him;[b] Elisha begged Elijah's permission to kiss his father and
mother good-bye before leaving to follow him.[c]

Other kisses are dead ends. Samuel kissed Saul when he
anointed him and sent the new king on toward Rachel's
sepulcher. David kissed Absalom. The people of Israel kissed
Absalom's hand. Joab took Amasa by the beard with his right
hand to kiss him, and slew him with the sword in his left hand.[d]

Consequential kisses punctuate greeting, meeting, going,
coming, embracing, falling on the neck, on the face, weeping,
smelling, and blessing. They are moments on the way. But only
between Naomi and her daughters-in-law, and at Jacob's first
encounter with Rachel, does anyone kiss, and raise the voice,
and weep.

In Ruth, this verbal constellation appears twice.

First, following the death of her sons in Moab, Naomi told
her daughters-in-law to return each to her own mother's house.
She, Naomi, will return alone to the land of Judah.

"Then she kissed them; and they lifted up their voice, and
wept."

Again, when Ruth and Orpah insisted on returning with her
to her people, Naomi mapped out the extent of her barrenness
and despair, concluding:

a. Exodus 18:7
b. 1Samuel 20:41; 2Samuel 19:39
c. 1Kings 19:18-20
d. 1Samuel 10:1-2; 2Samuel 14:33-15:5; 20:9-10

"'The hand of the LORD is gone out against me.'
And they lifted up their voice, and wept again:
and Orpah kissed her mother in law;
but Ruth clave unto her."[a]
The repetition forms a circle:
kiss, raise voice, weep : raise voice, weep, kiss
Definitions are also circular. Like negative electrons orbiting the positively charged nucleus, they trace an apparent shell, or meaning.

Some words mean one thing and its opposite at the same time, like "drug" which means both medicine and poison, or "cleave," which means both sunder and unite.

One daughter-in-law, Orpah, separates and departs from Naomi; the other, Ruth, joins her and departs with Naomi. The kiss of separation is also the kiss of kinship.

Were there even two separate moments, a before and after? Or does the second telling of the farewell emphasize, draw a circle around the kiss, rather than signal a repetition in time? Or both?

Holding even palpable opposites in mind at the same time is difficult; the attempt resembles a scale model of larger, more resistant mysteries, such as "God is one."

Despair is also desire.

The kiss-voice-weep verses in Ruth crown the first turn, act one of an extended drama. But Jacob's encounter with Rachel comes full stop. Events flow on either side of this first contact, which occupies an entire verse on its own.

Jacob caught sight of Rachel, unblocked the well's mouth, and watered Laban's sheep.

Next, Jacob kissed Rachel, and lifted his voice, and wept.

---

a. Ruth 1:9; 13-14

Then Jacob introduced himself to Rachel as her kinsman.

That kiss was a sign, akin to the stone pillar Jacob erected to his recognition of "that certain place" as the house of God and the gate of heaven, but made of breath. It proclaimed the renewal of the promise made to Abraham and Isaac. It marked the beginning of Jacob becoming Israel. That kiss, like light from darkness in the beginning, at first touch separated into love and loss, grief and joy, meeting and parting.

As for Jacob's raised voice, conceivably it sounded like the noise made by angels' wings as they kissed—that is, touched one another—in Ezekiel's vision.[a] Or perhaps the sound was Jacob touching Rachel's lips. His lifted voice and weeping were then aftersound.

The second Psalm advises us to
"Kiss the son, lest he be angry,
and ye perish from the way.
Blessed are all they that put their trust in him."
In another key, Psalm 85 records that
"Mercy and truth are met together;
righteousness and peace have kissed each other.
Truth shall spring out of the earth;
and righteousness look down from heaven."

God once smiled on Israel,
Returned them from captivity,
Forgotten and forgiven.
Now think of us, let us remember
More than anger, more than children
Heaped before their fathers.

---

a. Ezekiel 3:13

Speak us peace, and all who are not
Fools must listen. Blow one kiss
   And dandelions, truth
Will sprout through cracking sidewalks, wild
Puffballs, fierce and multiplying.
   The second kiss brings rain.[a]

---

a. Psalm 85

HE SENT
WRESTLING WITH ANGELS AND THE DUST
VA-YISHLAḤ/וישלח—Genesis 32:4-36:43
Jacob sent messengers before him to Esau his brother
to the land of Seir, the country of Edom.

Rashi says, "Jacob sent actual angels."

Maimonides[38] regards angels' existence as a fact. Everyone or any thing carrying out a divine order is an angel. Before they accomplish their mission, messengers are called men; afterwards, they are angels.

According to Rabbi Ishmael, Jacob had some inkling of his future, although he could not grasp it. Fleeing Esau, on the way to Padan-Aram Jacob fell asleep. There, he saw a ladder between earth and heaven with the angels of God ascending and descending. Jacob heard, "And, behold, I am with thee, and will keep thee," and called that place Beth-el.[39]

When Jacob returned to Canaan by the same way, angels met him, and Jacob saw them. Yet, approaching the country of his birth, Jacob sent messengers ahead to prepare his brother Esau, and was greatly afraid.

Ishmael wondered, "Would a man to whom God has given assurance be anxious? No. Jacob worried, 'What if God abandons me?'"[40]

Rabbi Simeon offered, "The righteous do not rely upon the intervention of angels, but rather on prayer and supplication. God frightened Jacob because he wanted to hear Jacob's prayer:

'God of my father Abraham, and God of my father Isaac—
the One who said to me,
"Return to your land, and kindred, and I will do you good"—
I am too small for all the kindnesses,
all the truth, which you have done your servant:

With just my rod I crossed over this Jordan;
and now I am become two camps.
'Deliver me, I pray, from the hand of my brother,
from the hand of Esau—
for I fear him, lest he come and strike me down,
mother and children.
'And you, you said: "I will surely do you good,
and make your seed as sea sand,
which cannot be counted by numbers."'

Ḥizkiyah asked, "If all those angels accompanied him, why was it written, 'Jacob was left alone?' He was not alone."

Rabbi Isaac answered, "They left him to wrestle with Samael, Esau's guardian angel, and confirm the blessings Isaac bestowed on Jacob. At the same time, two camps of messengers went off to sing in the heavenly choir."[41]

And there wrestled a man with him.

The Aramaic Targum, the Greek Septuagint, and the King James version translate Jacob's opponent, אִישׁ/ish, as "a man."

In *Jewish Antiquities,* Josephus matches Jacob against "a phantasm."

The Palestinian Targum renders his challenger as "an angel in the likeness of a man."

The Hebrew verb אָבַק/avaq [to wrestle] occurs only at this place in the Torah. The same root forms the noun "dust" which appears in Exodus, Deuteronomy, and Nahum.

The rabbis say: "He wrestled with him" implies that Jacob and the angel grappled face-to-face.

Rabbi Joshua said: "The dust of their feet whirled upward to the Throne of Glory, for it says, 'as he wrestled with him;'

and the prophet Nahum says, 'Clouds are the dust of His feet.'"[a]

Menahem explains that "there wrestled a man" means "and a man was dirtied," for their feet kicked up dust.

According to Berekiah Berabbi the Priest, the angel with whom Jacob wrestled by himself was as large as one third of the world.[42]

Rashi wrote: "He wrestled" means "He was tied."

Ein Yaakov records that the angel grappling with Jacob could not depart without Jacob's permission.

The angel begged, "Let me go; the day breaks."

Jacob retorted, "Are you a thief or gambler, that you fear the dawn?"

Two bands of passing angels called out,

"Michael! Up! Up! Time to sing[b]—

begin, or there will be no morning song."

Jacob said, "I will not let you go, unless you bless me."

The wrestler parried, "I am just the servant; you are the son. And you require my blessing?"

Jacob, "Nonetheless, I won't let go until you give me your name."

The angel answered, "Your name shall be called no more Jacob, but Israel."

Rabbi Eliezer took this message to mean that, when the angel called the man's name "Israel," he called him by his own name—Israel—which teaches that an angel's named according to its mission.

The angel closed with: "Bless you, born of woman, for you entered the palace above and live."[43]

The choir practice angels called Jacob's angel "Michael." Other

a. Nahum 1:3
b. Song of Songs 2:12

legends name Jacob's adversary "Gabriel." Some say Jacob fought with several angels.

An early Palestinian midrash identifies the angel as Sariel, "chief of those who praise," and an anagram for Israel. The same source interprets Peniel, Jacob's name for the place where he extracted the blessing from his antagonist, as "I have seen the angels of God face-to-face."

The name Israel is variously explained: as "the man who saw God"; as "trying to sing instead of the angels;" or, as "joyful like the angels at the time of their singing."

Israel also means "the remnant of God;" or, "he who walks straight with God;" as opposed to Jacob—"he who walks crookedly."[44]

Rashi notes that the angel only foretold Jacob's change of name. He did not effect it. The angel told the patriarch that, at the assigned moment, the One will show himself to you. "At Beth-el God will meet us; there he will speak with us and call your name Israel. And I will be there, to confirm the blessings for you." "There" would be the time to come:

in Canaan, below Beth-el, where Jacob buried his mother's nurse at the Oak of Weeping;

by the wayside when departing Beth-el, where Jacob buried Rachel, lost in childbirth;

in Mamre, where he and Esau buried Isaac, where Abraham entertained three men on their way to Sodom and Gomorrah, and where Sarah laughed.

The fool says to himself, What God?
And takes, and breaks his word, and does
No good, no, none, not anyone. Such rot
In fruit would sicken flies.

God peered down through his window
In the sky, to see his children
At their lives, the men and women,
To find if even one still tried to know

Life and good from death and evil,
But they'd all gone back to witches'
Days, and gold greed blood haphazard couples
And no one knows, does, good, or teaches.

Don't they have an inkling of their doing,
Dying without shame and chewing
Up the people (who would, could they, love
The lore) like bakers' crusty loaves?

The bad have not called God by any name, not even
When the fear came on them, fear that floats
Like bone ash puffed by chimneys in the air, spouts
Of naked ignorance despised shamed by no God.

If only someone would save us from
The blind, our selves, the bloated, come
He from Jerusalem or nearer home
To sunder what has hindered us
From freedom and from happiness,
Then Israel, who wrestled, shall rejoice.[a]

---

a. Psalm 53

HE DWELT
WHO OWNS THE DREAM? AND ITS INTERPRETATION?

VA-YESHEV/וישב—Genesis 37:1-40:23
Jacob dwelt in the land wherein his father was a stranger,
in the land of Canaan.

Through Joel, God proclaims that, in the day of the LORD:
> I will pour out my spirit on all flesh;
> Your sons and daughters shall prophesy;
> Your old men shall dream dreams,
> And your young men shall see visions.[a]

"Dream," (as noun and verb, חָלַם/חֲלֹם/ḥalam/ḥalom) appears more times in this portion than anywhere else in the Bible.

Of the dreamers in Genesis, Abimelech and Laban hear unequivocal voices, while Jacob and Joseph have visions (marked by הִנֵּה/hinneh [Behold!])—dreams understood directly by both the dreamer and, in Joseph's case, by those to whom the dream is told.

Pharaoh's servants and, later, Pharaoh, also have dream visions. Even though their written language is hieroglyphic, they do not understand what's pictured in their dreams.

What is a dream?

The Zohar reveals that, when night falls, the gates of the demon world open.

The gates of the heart, which is Eden, close.

Those gates, the eyes, are lidded so that demons cannot look into them and usurp light in the heart.

At night the soul sends its spirit on a mission like Noah's dove from the sealed ark. The spirit flies from place to place, according to one's failings.

---

a. Joel 3:1

The good soul is met by Ezekiel and all the four-faced winged powers. They lead it to where the spirits of living creatures of the Throne stand and wheel. There the sleeper sees visions, imaginary sights, prophetic spectacles—which is why the rabbis say a dream is one-sixtieth part of prophecy.

Isaac's blessing upon Jacob takes the form of a prophecy: "Let peoples serve thee and nations bow down to thee.

Be lord over thy brethren,

and let thy mother's sons bow down to thee."[a]

And, the Torah notes, Esau hated Jacob because of the blessing.[b]

Urged by his mother, Jacob departed Beersheba toward Haran. Stopping in a place for the night, he dreamed a vision:

Behold!, a ladder between heaven and earth,

with the messengers of God ascending and descending.

Jacob awoke and said,

"Surely the Name is in this place, and I knew it not."[c]

In the fourth volume of the instructional book written for his son which compiles all that was known in Classical times about the interpretation of dreams, the second century Greek Artemidorus explains that "in regard to the way in which dreams come true, brothers have the same meaning as enemies, and enemies as brothers."

Rabbi Banaah reported: "Jerusalem was home to twenty-four interpreters of dreams. Once I dreamed a dream and went to all of them, and not one agreed with the other in the reading of my dream, yet all their interpretations were fulfilled, confirming the saying: All dreams follow the utterances of

a. Genesis 27:29
b. Genesis 27:41
c. Genesis 28:10-16

the mouth."

In Sigmund Freud's *Interpretation of Dreams*, the true reading comes from the dreamer, not from the one to whom the dream is told.

Like Jacob his father, Joseph was hated by his brothers.

Like Jacob, Joseph had dream visions.

His first dream, of their sheaves bowing down to him in the field, he told to his brothers.

They answered with the dream's interpretation—"Shalt thou indeed reign over us? or shalt thou indeed have dominion over us?"—a repetition of the blessing Jacob stole from Esau.[a]

When Joseph related his second vision (of the sun and moon and eleven stars), Jacob interpreted the dream as a question: "Shall I and thy mother and thy brethren indeed come to bow down to thee to the earth?"

Like the rest of creation, the seed of dreams is desire, and the fruit is speech.

In Egypt's prison, Pharaoh's butler and baker told Joseph that they looked sad because they each had dreamed a dream, and none could interpret it.

Joseph replied: "Do not interpretations belong to God?" He then interpreted the butler's dream for good, and the baker's for ill. Joseph asked the butler to remember him when he was restored to Pharaoh's favor.

But the chief butler forgot Joseph.

Rabbi Simeon explained that "An uninterpreted dream is like an unread letter" means:

the dream will be fulfilled, even without being disclosed, because the dream has its own power;

---

a. Genesis 27:29

also, the dream must be remembered below, or it will be forgotten above;

also, a dream is an unripe form of prophecy."

As for revelation, Amos declares, "God will do nothing without revealing it to his prophets."[a]

Without prophets, ask the Sages what things mean;
when sages lack, there remain the intimations of a dream;
should dreams fail, look to the sky and read the flight of birds.

A dream is not substantial, like matter or the word.

So Jeremiah warns against those prophets "who think
by dreams to cause my people to forget my Name."[b]

Beyond a certain age, one realizes he won't live forever;
beyond another age, a person may not want to.

Then there's the wish that one might be delivered,
if not from mortality then perhaps from disappointment:

the hope that what was never even thought about in dreams
could not be so;

the recognition that something dreamed has come to pass,
but not as in the dream.

Rabbi Judah and Rabbi Yose were walking.
Yose remembered how his father told him
Years before that, in the very place
They had just left, in his sixtieth year
Yose would find a treasure. "I now am sixty,"
Yose said, "but have not found the treasure.
Could it be the words we have just spoken
Are the treasure that my father meant?"
Rabbi Judah stopped and could not answer.

a. Amos 3:7
b. Jeremiah 23:27-28

Yose turned aside into a cave.
In the dark, between two rocks, he found
A book, which he brought out into the light.
Opening the book, Yose saw
Rubbings of the seventy-two letters
Given Adam, by which means he knew
All the higher and the lower wisdom,
All that would occur up to the end
Of time. As the scholars ventured deeper
Into Adam's aleph-beth, a fire
Wind plucked the book out of their hands.

The two walked on to Simeon ben Yoḥai,
And told him of the wisdom they discovered.
"Perhaps you were looking at those letters
That tell when the Messiah's time will come?"
He asked. They could not answer Simeon,
Because they had forgotten all they'd read.
"Ah," said their teacher. "The holy One
Does not permit these things to be revealed
Now, but when the time is near at hand
Nothing will be hidden. Little children
Will sport with wisdom yet undreamed by us,
And tell true stories of the world to come."

AT THE END
JOSEPH, AND THE EXPLANATION OF HIDDEN THINGS

MIKKETS/מִקֵּץ—Genesis 41:1-44:17
It came to pass at the end of two full years,
that Pharaoh dreamed:
and, Behold! he stood by the river.

According to Rabbi Judah,[45] the Creator called humans "complainers and the children of complainers.

"To my face, Adam complained about his other half after both had eaten the forbidden fruit; Jacob complained that his way was hidden from the LORD,[a] even while I made his son governor over Egypt."

Simeon the son of Yoḥai understood that every matter from God's mouth comes in a measure,[46] and everything created has an end:

"The Almighty set a limit to the sun, a boundary to the heavens and the earth, an edge to darkness.

"God made a time for Israel's journey out of Egypt, and set a term on Joseph's time in prison: At the end of two years.

"'At the end' is a place without remembering.

"After reading the chief butler's dream, Joseph said: 'Remember me when all goes well for you,'[b] thinking Pharaoh's servant dreamed about remembering.

"In darkness, from a place forgotten, Joseph relied upon another man.

"At the end, where things are understood, after two years of forgetting were fulfilled, Pharaoh's man remembered Joseph."

Rabbi Eliezer counted ten kings who ruled the world from one

---

a. Isaiah 40:2
b. Genesis 40:14

end to the other: the third was Joseph, and the fourth, Solomon.

Solomon's proverb about the poor but wise child, "Out of prison he comes forth to rule,"[a] Rav Kahana applied to Joseph: "In the famine, all nations came to Egypt to buy food. Joseph spoke to each according to their different tongues, and understood their speech, their seventy languages, like Solomon after him.

"Except with his brothers: for them he used a translator."

Joseph knew his brethren, but they knew him not because, when they sold him twenty-two years before, Joseph had no beard, so they bowed down before the governor of Egypt.

The sight of his brothers bowing to him, faces to the earth, reminded Joseph of dreams from his youth—of sheaves and of the sun and moon and stars. Prophetically inspired, Joseph saw his dream fulfilled, and then remembered it.[47]

Likewise, when Joseph's brothers denied that they were spies, saying "We are all the sons of one man," the spirit of prophecy kindled within them.

"Unknowingly," Rashi observed, "they included Joseph among their father's sons, a truth still hidden from them."

After placing him over Egypt, and giving him an Egyptian wife, Pharaoh named Joseph Zaphenath-paneaḥ, Egyptian for "He explains hidden things."

Tradition holds that, in the beginning, the heaven and the earth spooled out and out like two endless clews of warp thread, until God rebuked the pillars of heaven and brought all to a standstill.

Resh Laqish interpreted the verse

---

a. Ecclesiastes 4:14

I am אֵל שַׁדַּי/El Shaddai—God Almighty[a]

to mean:

"I am He that said to the world: דַּי/dai—Enough!"[48]

When Jacob sent his sons back to Egypt with Benjamin, he told them: "God Almighty give you mercy.

"May the One who told the heavens and the earth, Enough!

set a limit to my suffering and say, 'Enough.'

"Now you lack nothing, save prayer.

"Behold, I pray for you."

Commentators argue that, when Jacob prayed, "May the man release your other brother and Benjamin to you," by "other brother" the patriarch meant Simeon. But the prophetic Spirit glowed in him as it had within his ten sons, and Jacob included Joseph unawares.

Rabbi Phineḥas adds: "As one standing before the judge cries out, Jacob prayed:

'May He who will say "Enough" to suffering to come say "Enough" to mine.'"[49]

A psalm directs:

"Let every person pray to You

at a time You can be found."[b]

What time is that?

Abba said: "Old age.

"Pray that when old your eyes can see,

your mouth will chew, your feet still walk,

for at the end these things depart."[50]

Guilt hidden
Maddens.

a. Genesis 17:1; 35:11
b. Psalm 32

Madness:
The affront
To sense.
Innocence:
The lash, or
Rumor
Spurring
Candor.
Unbending
Oaks crack,
Willows
Beside rivers
Hardly ever.[a]

In answer to his prayer, God told Jacob: "See the miracles I will do for your children when I bring them out of Egypt."

Then Jacob saw his account was closed, and spoke the blessing: "God Almighty give you mercy."

Rabbi Ḥiyya closed his remarks with Solomon's saying: 'Hope deferred is sickness of heart,

but a desire come true is a tree of life.'[b]

"Desire is the ark of prayers," Ḥiyya said, "and bears them to the Presence, where they may be fulfilled.

"Hope deferred, like Jacob's wish for Joseph, passes from hand to hand among those with the power to destroy, but the prayers of those who remember and keep suffer no delay."

Joseph remembered, and asked for,

then raised his eyes and saw, and kept

Benjamin, his brother, his mother's son.

---

a. Psalm 32
b. Proverbs 13:12

HE CAME NEAR
THE DISTANCE BETWEEN THE ORIGINAL AND ITS TRANSLATION,
BETWEEN THE KNOWER AND THE KNOWN

VA-YIGGASH/ויגש—Genesis 44:18-47:27
Then Judah came near to him, and said:
Oh my lord, Let thy servant, I pray thee, speak a word...;
For you are like Pharaoh.

Maimonides distinguishes between the concrete and the abstract meanings of the Hebrew verb "to come near."

The primary sense of coming near applies to the motion of one body toward another, as when Judah came near to Joseph, or when Joseph made himself known to his brothers who could not recognize him and said, "Come near, I pray you." And they came near.

The other kind, which the philosopher characterizes as the cognitive coming near, identifies the union of a known thing with the knower. It pertains to inspiration and prophetic trance, as when the LORD said of Jerusalem:

"This people draw near with their mouth,
and with their lips they honor me,
but have removed their heart far from me,
and their fear of me is taught by rote, by men."[a]

It makes no difference, Maimonides concluded, whether one is at the center of the earth or in the highest sphere of heaven—he is no farther from God here than there—since nearness consists of apprehending him, and distance from God is the lot of one who knows him not.

The distance between an original phrase and its translation into another tongue sometimes turns the right word in the dictionary sense into the wrong idea. Maimonides admired

a. Isaiah 29:13

Onkelos the Convert's determination to forestall any suggestion that God has a physical body. In his Aramaic version of the Five Books of Moses, whenever Onkelos encountered a passage indicating movement on God's part, he translated it as the manifestation and appearance of a created light. So, when the LORD came down upon Mount Sinai in Exodus,[a] the Convert renders the Hebrew "descended" as "manifested;" God's investigation of Sodom and Gomorrah—"I will descend now and see"—becomes in Aramaic "I will manifest myself now and see."

However, the Aramaic translates God's assurance to Jacob—"I will go down with you into Egypt"—word-for-word. Here, God spoke to Joseph's father in the visions of the night, so the passage records what was said, not things of the imagination.[51]

The rabbis differ. One said "Judah came near" for battle; another said, for conciliation. The Sages ruled that "coming near" applies to prayer, but Rabbi Leazar said it was all one: battle, conciliation, prayer.

When Joseph seized Benjamin, he told his brothers, "The man with whom the goblet is found will be my bondman; the rest of you, go up to your father in peace."

Then Judah approached Joseph, saying, "You take Benjamin, and think there will be peace in my father's house? Take me, Oh my lord, not him.

"You do us wrong. You said, 'Bring him down to me, that I may set eyes upon him.'

"Is this setting eyes on him, to take him hostage?

"Let my words enter your ears. Pharaoh took this youth's

a. Exodus 19:11, 20

grandmother for a single night, and he and his house were smitten with plagues.

"Beware lest you be cursed.

"How shall I go up to my father if the last son of his old age is left behind?"

Joseph said, "Come near. Debate the matter. State your case."

Judah said, "From the start, you falsely accused us. First you called us spies; second you said we came to find out where the land is weak; third you claimed we stole the goblet.

"You are like Pharaoh:
Pharaoh promises and then defaults—as do you;
Pharaoh has a taste for young men like our brother—so do you.

"Yes, Pharaoh is a king and you are second to him, but my father is a king in Canaan, and I am second to him.

"How many peoples have come down to Egypt to buy food? Did you question them as you questioned us? Did we ask for your daughter, or offer you our sister? Yet we hid nothing."

Joseph said, "Judah, why do you speak for your brothers? Surely you are not the first-born."

Judah answered, "I assured my father I would stand for Benjamin, should you demand to keep him."

Joseph asked, "With what did you offer? Silver? Gold? I will give it."

Judah: "Not my substance, but my soul—it will be outcast in the world to come should my brother not return.

"What do you require from Benjamin? Greatness?
I am greater; strength? I am stronger. Take me.

"Better I should be your slave, than say…. Say what? What could I tell our father?"

Joseph: "Say, 'The rope follows the bucket.'"

Judah: "You swear by the power of Pharaoh, but I swear by my father's God, that if I draw my sword, I will begin with you, and finish with Pharaoh."

Rabbi Yudan commented that, when Judah grew angry, two hairs protruded from his heart and ripped through his clothes. To stoke his anger, he would fill his leather belt with bean-sized copper pieces and grind them with his teeth.

Had Judah started his threat with Pharaoh and ended with Joseph, Joseph would have held his peace. But Judah menaced Joseph, so the second man in all of Egypt nodded to his son Manasseh, who stamped his foot, and made the palace shake.

Judah thought, "Such a stomp! just like the line of Jacob." And he began to speak more gently.

Judah: "You play us false."

Joseph: "So false as when you sold your brother?"

Judah: "I will paint Egypt with blood."

Joseph: "Like you painted your brother's coat, and told your father that a beast tore him to pieces?"

Judah: "And you would take from him the child of his old age, and have sorrow bring our gray-haired father to the grave?"

Judah answered Joseph, word for word, and each time he mentioned Jacob, he pierced Joseph's heart.

Rabbi Ḥiyya added, "All the words spoken by Judah to Joseph were to appease Joseph, and his brothers, and Benjamin."[52]

Then Joseph could not restrain himself.

He cleared the place of attendants, stood alone before his brothers, and said, "Did you not tell me this lad had a brother? Well, I bought him.

"I will call, and he will show himself to you:
'Joseph son of Jacob, come here. Joseph, come out.
Speak with your brothers who sold you into Egypt.'"
  (The brothers searched every corner of the house.)
  Joseph asked, "What do you see?"
  His brothers: "We see no one. Only you."
  He asked again, "Why look here or there? Come near.
I am your brother Joseph."
  (They could say nothing.)
  "Look! your eyes can see, as do my brother Benjamin's,
that I speak with my own mouth, in Hebrew,
  what I feel with my heart."
  (Still they did not believe him.)
  Then Joseph said: "Come close."
As they approached, he kissed them, and he wept.[53]

HE LIVED
THE FEAR OF GOD

VA-YEḤI/ויחי—Genesis 47:28-50:26
Jacob lived in the land of Egypt seventeen years:
so the whole age of Jacob was one hundred forty-seven years.

What is the fear of God?

Rabbi Nehuniah answered, "The first light."

When God said, "Let there be light, and there was light,"
he did not say, "and it was so." The light was so intense that no
created thing could gaze upon it. So, God stored the first light
in a place apart, to reveal to the righteous in the world to come.

From one thousandth of that radiance God made a precious
stone which contained all the commandments. Its power was
beauty, one measure of all things.

Abraham came. God offered him this stone, but Abraham
did not want it, and instead chose kindness.

Isaac came. He also refused beauty, and took up strength,
or holy terror, as his possession.

Then Jacob came. He wanted the radiant stone, but was
denied it. Instead, he received the blessings of his fathers plus
his own gift: truth and peace.

And this is the complete inheritance of Jacob.[54]

In Hebrew, there are two words for "I."

The simple first-person pronoun אֲנִי/ani means "the self."

The other heightened, eternal intense singular, אָנֹכִי/anochi
might be understood as one word, "only-I." It is used when God
speaks of himself, or promises, or when someone swears a
solemn oath.

The only-I connects above to here below.

Jacob, waiting for his father's blessing, answered dim-eyed

Isaac's question, "Who are you, my son?" with "Only-I, Esau, your firstborn."

When God appeared to Jacob in his dream and promised, "Only-I with you," Jacob woke, and feared, and said, "Dreadful this place, the house of God, the gate of Heaven;" and vowed, "If God will be with me, and will keep me in this way that only-I go, then the LORD will be my God."

This chapter opens "Jacob lived." In Torah, "he lived" is the herald of "he died."

The patriarch asked Joseph to inter him in the burial place of his fathers, and Joseph swore, "I will do as you have said."

And after blessing Joseph's children, Israel told his son who ruled all Egypt: "Only-I die; But God will bring you back to the land of your fathers."

Jacob then called his other sons together and, according to tradition, gave them this sign:

"God said to my grandfather: 'I am your shield.' The same 'I' spoke to my father Isaac. He also said to me, 'Only-I am the God of Beth-el; I will go with you into Egypt.'

"If One comes and says to you 'אָנֹכִי/anochi—I am,' know it is your God.

"If not, that is not God."

So, when the children of Israel stood before Sinai, the holy One began by saying "אָנֹכִי/anochi," and they knew God.

His sons carried Jacob's embalmed body into Canaan, and buried him in the cave of Machpelah beside Leah along with Abraham and Sarah, Isaac and Rebekah, and (some say) Adam and Eve.

Joseph and his brothers returned to Egypt. There, the brothers feared that with their father dead, Joseph would now exact revenge for the treachery in Shechem.

But Joseph reassured them, asking,

"Am I myself in place of God?" and told them,

"Fear not, Only-I will sustain you and your little ones."

According to Rabbi Judah, here the eternal pronoun expresses love. And here, Rabbi Nehemiah said, the personal pronoun "I" inspires fear, inspires awe.[55]

Joseph lived 110 years, and (echoing Israel) said, "I die, but God will surely remember you, and you will carry my bones up from Egypt."

So Joseph died, and they embalmed him.

In one Exodus legend, while the children of Israel busied themselves with the spoils of Egypt, Moses searched for Joseph's casket. Asher's daughter Serah (who lived in Joseph's generation) remembered that after embalming him, the Egyptians put Joseph in a metal coffin and sank it in the Nile.

Moses walked down to the riverbank and called out: "Joseph, Joseph. Now is the time meant by God when he said, 'I will redeem you.'

"The Name awaits. If you show yourself, well and good. If not, we are free of the oath to carry you up from Egypt."

The river burbled, and Joseph's ark floated to the surface.

All the years they wandered the Wilderness, the Israelites carried Joseph's casket alongside the Ark of the Presence. They buried Joseph's bones in Shechem, where he sought his brothers, who sold him to a caravan of merchants.

Rabbi Eleazar observed: "Even if a person lives a thousand years, on the day that he departs from the world, it seems to him as if he only lived a single day."

Eleazar asked his father Rabbi Simeon, "Since it is revealed that human beings die, why does God bring souls down to the world? Why does He need this?"

His father answered, "This question has been asked in every generation.

"I say, the One has souls descend into this world to make his presence known, and gathers them up after.

"The need for it, there is the mystery."[56]

Ludwig Wittgenstein eschewed the why of it by saying, "A question with no answer's not a question."

And King Lear, when Cordelia gave no answer, snapped, "Nothing comes of nothing. Speak again."

What then of one who answers with a question? Who asks and answers, "Who am I?"

I said,
    I will watch my mouth
And made no comment even
On the good, and I was sad.
My heart raced, something hot
Inside me made me cry out loud:
God, let me know when I've begun
A thing, and when it will be done;
Let me know how my days will run
From hot and fat to dim, to fail
And fall without a flutter by your hand.
What's there to wait for? Money? Power?
What's there to hope for? Old age? Honor?
The mock of dimwits? Spoiled children?
Your finger pressed across my mouth.
My lovely self was flannel, time a moth.

Hear me. Don't be put off by tears.
I'm stranger and a nomad like my father.
Give me strength enough to rise, to speak,
To spill a glass of water on the tabletop before
I thirst, and sip, and am no more.[a]

---

a. Psalm 39

Exodus

NAMES

MOSES'S OTHER NAMES, HOW GOD IS CALLED, AND
WHAT PHARAOH FOUND IN HIS ARCHIVES

SHEMOT/שמות—Exodus 1:1-6:1
These are the names of the children of Israel
which came into Egypt with Jacob;
every man coming with his household.

Counted in their lifetime,[a] and again after they died, God
Collects the scattered, castoff, brokenhearted seed of Israel,
Knows how many stars there are,
And calls them all by name, and hears the answer.[b]

Pharaoh's daughter loved the Hebrew child as if he were her
own,
"And she called his name Moses:
Because I drew him from the water."
Rabbi Joshua the Palestinian says God told Pharaoh's
daughter:
"Moses was not yours, yet you called him your son.
You are not mine, yet I will call you Bathiah, God's daughter."
Moses had nine other names: Jered, Heber, Jekuthiel, Abi
Gedor, Abi Soco, Abi Zanoah, also Tobiah, because he was
good, and Shemaiah, because God heard his prayer and,
Tanḥuma said, he was called Levi, after his tribe.
With Moses, that makes ten.
Nonetheless, throughout the Torah Moses is known only by
the name Pharaoh's daughter gave him; even God called him by
no other.
Moses led his father-in-law Jethro's flock to the far end of

a. Genesis 46:8 ff
b. Psalm 147

75

the Wilderness, to the Mountain of God. It was also called:
Bashan, because God came there; the Mount of Peaks, where
God revealed himself; Mount Moriah, where God desired to
dwell; Horeb, where the sword of judgment was
unsheathed;and Sinai, because there God declared idolators
hateful to him, and pronounced their doom.

When God came down to deliver Israel from the hand of
the Egyptians, he abandoned the mountain and entered a thorn
bush, an emblem of grief and distress, where the angel of the
LORD appeared to Moses in a flame of fire.
 Rabbi Yoḥanan said, "This was Michael."
 Rabbi Ḥanina differed. "No. Gabriel. The flame gave
Moses courage, so when he saw the fires on Sinai, he would not
be afraid."
 "And he looked and, behold, the bush burned with fire
  and the bush was not consumed."
From this verse, the Babylonian sages have determined that
heavenly flame branches upwards, burns but does not consume,
and is black, while earthly fire burns in sheets, is red, consumes
and burns.

Moses said, "I will turn aside and see this great sight."
 Yoḥanan said, "Moses took five steps aside."
 Simeon the son of Laqish thought he turned his face to see.
 Another claimed that, when God saw Moses did not stop his
work to gawk, He knew the man was worthy to shepherd Israel,
 "And He said: 'Moses Moses.'"
 God also called Abraham, Jacob and Samuel twice by name,
but their names are separated by a pause, a comma.
 Not so Moses.

With other prophets, God spoke at intervals.
With Moses God discoursed continuously.
Simeon ben Yoḥai hears in "Moses Moses" love and urgency.[57]
Maimonides emphasizes that, while God directed Abraham, Isaac and Jacob in their private affairs, Moses was the first prophet to claim God called him, and sent him on a mission to all Israel.

Moses asked, "When I say to the Israelites:
'The God of your fathers has sent me to you,'
and they ask, 'What is His name?' what shall I say?"
God replied, "I Am that I Am
[אֶהְיֶה אֲשֶׁר אֶהְיֶה/ehyeh asher ehyeh].
"Tell them 'I Am [אֶהְיֶה/ehyeh] sent me to you.'"
In a midrash, the Immeasurable gave a longer answer:
"You want to know my name?
"When I judge created beings I am God;
when waging war against the wicked I am LORD of Hosts;
when I suspend judgment I am El Shaddai, Almighty God;
when I show mercy I am Adonai.
"I Am that I Am, I Am named by what I do.
I am what I was and I will be.
"When I will, an angel who is one third of creation
stretches out his hand from heaven and touches earth;
at my behest my messengers sit under a tree;
when I desire, my glory fills the world;
when moved, I spoke to Job out of the whirlwind;
and when I want to, I speak from a thorn bush."[58]
A poet and a pilgrim, Judah Halevi derived "I Am" from the Tetragrammaton, or from the root הָיָה/hayah [to be]. "It

prevents," he wrote, "the mind from pondering the incomprehensible real.

"So, when God told Moses 'I Am that I Am,' that Name means: 'the existing one, existing for you whenever you seek me. Let them search for no stronger proof than my presence among them, and name me accordingly. I will be with you—I have sent you, and I am with you everywhere.'"[59]

The Aristotelian Maimonides observed that, in Hebrew, there is no difference between saying "he was" and "he existed." The secret lives in the repetition of "I Am," which makes the subject identical with the predicate: a thing that exists and had to be before and after, a name with no attributes except existence.[60]

Moses argued the fitness of his call before the One: "Who? only I alone? Did you not promise Jacob
   'Only-I will go down with you into Egypt,
      and Only-I will bring you up again.'[a]
Now you say: 'Go to Pharaoh and bring Israel out of Egypt.'[61]

"Master of the World, if I, a prophet the son of a prophet, accept your decision with misgivings, how will Pharaoh, evil son of an evil one, heed my command?"

God answered, "You, will speak the holy language like my angels do, and Aaron your brother will speak words in Egyptian,[62] which I put in his mouth."

One legend tells that Moses and Aaron came before the royal court on the day Pharaoh received ambassadors. After the foreign dignitaries finished offering praise and gifts, Moses and Aaron stood in the entry.

Pharaoh asked, "Who are you?"

---

a. Genesis 46:3-4

They replied, "Men of the LORD God of Israel."

Pharaoh said, "What do you want?"

They told Pharaoh, "Thus says the LORD God of Israel:
'Let my people go.'"

Pharaoh said, "Who is the LORD, that I should listen to him? Instead of gifts, you offer words?"

Ḥama son of Ḥanina remarked: "A marvelous thing, speech of the lips: it equals the creation of the world."

Samuel son of Naḥman agreed. "A complicated power. Consider what the tongue can do:

"Sometimes a man must curl his tongue, and sometimes he must push his tongue against his teeth to make a certain sound.

"To pronounce a single Hebrew word, the one in Ezekiel[a] translated as 'according to your ways,' the tongue assumes eleven successive positions."[63]

Pharaoh searched his archives for the LORD God of Israel, but did not find the Name among the gods of Egypt or the other kingdoms.

Pharaoh said, "I know not the LORD,
neither will I let Israel go."

Moses and Aaron answered, "Fool.
You look for the Living God among the dead?

"You know him not?

"One day you will cry out:
'I have sinned against the LORD your God.'

"As for letting go, the day will come when you will say that, were old Jacob our father still alive, you would personally have packed his things, and let him go."[64]

---

a. Ezekiel 20:44

I APPEARED

WHY ARE PEOPLE SO BADLY TREATED?

VA-'ERA'/וארא—Exodus 6:2-9:35
God spoke to Moses, and said to him:
I am the LORD;
I appeared to Abraham, to Isaac, and to Jacob
as El Shaddai, God Almighty, but by my Name [יהוה]
I was not known to them.

Rabbi Akiba suggested that only one frog plagued Egypt, but it reproduced so rapidly that frogs filled the entire land. Eleazar ben Azariah rebuked him, asking what business Akiba had with stories. Better he should illuminate the difficult laws about touching an unclean thing.[65]
Why exert yourself in matters known to everyone?

Israel's deliverance begins with God's response to Moses' pointed query:
"Wherefore have you dealt so ill with this people?"
"Why have you sent me?"
The Name predicated—
"Now you will see what I will do;"[a]
then elaborated—
"[אֲנִי יְהוָה/ani ....] I am The LORD."

Va-yera is the first-person singular form of the verb רָאָה/ raah [to see]. The Hebrew root also translates as appear, perceive, look or look at, consider, heed, discern, reflect, be visible, cause to see, behold, experience.
One day, Rabbi Simeon sat with his son, Rabbi Eleazar.
Eleazar said, "It is written: 'I appeared to Abraham, to

---

a. Exodus 5:22-23

Isaac, and to Jacob.' Why 'I appeared'?

"The verse should read 'I spoke.'" That is, revelation comes in words we hear, not through the eye.

Rabbi Simeon replied, "Eleazar, it is a mystery.

"Some colors are seen, and some are not.

"An infinity of colors remained hidden until the Patriarchs saw them. The verse says 'I appeared' because at that time God's finite colors were revealed.

"The higher colors—concealed and unseen—no human has perceived, except for Moses."[66]

Moses saw, and heard, and spoke.

Through Aaron he told Israel that God has heard their groans in bondage, will bring them out from Egypt, redeem them, take them for his own, and bring them into the land promised to Abraham, to Isaac, and to Jacob.

Commanded to tell Pharaoh "Let my people go," Moses replied that even the children of Israel have not heard him.

"How then shall Pharaoh hearken unto me, who am of uncircumcised lips?"

Uncircumcised, according to Rashi, here means "closed, or impeded"—a usage painful to imagine.

To lend imagination time, the story pauses for a fourteen-verse genealogy of that Moses and Aaron, to whom the LORD said: "Bring out the children from the land of Egypt." Their interview then resumes where it left off, in Egypt, on the day God spoke to Moses, saying, "I am the LORD:

Speak to Pharaoh king of Egypt all that I say to you."

And Moses wondered,

"How shall Pharaoh hearken unto me?"

The matter of Pharaoh's hearkening gets answered in eight

chapters. The Name caused all to see, in Moses' words, through Aaron's mouth, by signs, in plagues, in wonders, from the river Nile's water turned to blood to Pharaoh's army drowned in the Red Sea.

Moses' prior question, concerning God's treatment of Israel, hangs fire. For those inclined to quarrel with what appears to be unseen, perhaps the answer can be found wherever it hides. A rabbinic axiom maintains that what is revealed belongs to us; what is concealed belongs to God. So, if there be an answer to why people are so badly treated, it must be found in us.

> What made all the earth has been
> Forgotten even by the ones disposed to know.
> Perhaps a list of what was done for Jacob's children helps?
> The Red Sea parted, they crossed dry shod,
> Following the smoke and fire pillar placed before them.
> Stranger prophets could not curse them.
> Basic appetites would test them, thirst and hunger
> Make them falter, long for Egypt's slave abundance.
> Forty years a generation wandered looking backward,
> > disappeared.

> I appear before the book God gave to Moses
> With full hands, with promises, made when
> I could not know I would be able, kept:
> The ox, the goat, the lamb, the song of praise.
> God heard the music of my heart. I leapt.[a]

---

a. Psalm 66

GO

BO'/בא—Exodus 10:1-13:16
And the LORD said to Moses: Go to Pharaoh;
for I have hardened his heart, and the heart of his servants,
that I might show these My signs among them.

God commanded Moses: "Go."

Using the same imperative, God told Noah: "Come."[a]
Rashi noted that the Torah did not need to start
"In the beginning..." It also can start at
"This month shall be unto you the beginning of months."
The liturgical calendar was created by these words, which introduce the first commandment given to Israel, the Passover offering.

Over twenty-six generations counting from the sixth day of Creation until the day Israel went forth from Egypt, no one spoke the words "Praise the LORD." That prayer was first uttered on the night Egypt's first-born were smitten, while Israel slaughtered their Passover sacrifices.

That night, Pharaoh came to Moses and Aaron and told them, "Rise up, get you forth from among my people."

They answered, "At night? Are we thieves that we go forth by night? "We will leave in the morning."

Pharaoh said: "By then, all Egypt will be dead. Go now, and bless me also."

Bless, really? Pharaoh meant: "Pray for me, that I not die. I am a first-born."[67]

---

a. Genesis 7:1

Two plagues of darkness preceded the Passover night.

The eighth plague, locusts, covered the face—strictly speaking, the [עַיִן/ayin] eye—of the whole earth, so that the land was darkened. An east wind [רוּחַ/ruaḥ] blew day and night, like God's breath upon the waters while darkness covered the face of the deep. Next morning, the wind brought locusts.

The ninth plague was a darkness which may be felt, the same darkness God divided from the light. One legend links felt darkness to the grope of Moses' curse upon the heedless in Deuteronomy: "You shall grope at noonday, as the blind grope in darkness."[a]

Rashi clarifies that "in Egypt, darkness was doubled and redoubled so thick until there was in it substance that could be felt."

Felt how?

In 1158, Abraham ibn Ezra travelled to England. There, he wrote, "a thick darkness comes over the Atlantic Ocean. In that fog it is impossible to tell day from night. The fog sometimes lasts for five days. I have been in it many times."

Rashi says there were again three other days of darkness, twice as thick as before, so dense that no one moved: he who sat could not stand up, and he who stood could not sit down.

In that palpable obscure, those Israelites who chose not to go out from Egypt died.

The multitude who exited Egypt differed from those who perished in the darkness in three respects. According to Eliezer:

> they did not change their language;
> they did not change their names;
> they did not slander one another.

---

a. Deuteronomy 28:29

Moses, who bore an Egyptian name, prophesied to Pharaoh,
"Thus saith the LORD:
'About midnight will I go out into the midst of Egypt:
And all the firstborn in the land shall die.'"
By "about midnight" Moses meant "before or after."

But, as Albert Einstein put it, "God does not play dice, and when the Old One speaks, he is precise."

It came to pass at midnight. At—not by the clock, the stroke of twelve.

There was no clock.

How then to place a finger at mid-darkness?

One legend hangs David's harp in his bedroom window. At midnight, the north wind blew across the strings. That music woke the king who rose up, studied until dawn, and sang.

Rabbi Yose asked, "Why pass over at midnight? Why not by day, so all could see?

"And why slaughter all those weaklings, all those lambs? Why not just commanders and the warriors?"

The School of Elijah connects the slaying of Egypt's firstborn with Pharaoh's order to the midwives that they kill all male children born to the Hebrews. The midwives disobeyed, but God considered the decree as though it had been carried out.

This, their commentary explains, is a difference between Israel and the nations. The peoples of the world are held accountable for an evil thought, as though it had been carried out. But Israel are not judged until the evil deed has actually been committed.

Rabbi Simeon answered half of Rabbi Yose's question. "Our festivals, holidays, and Sabbaths, all our observances recall God's bringing Israel out of Egypt. That going forth is the base and root of Torah, its commandments, our entire faith.

"So, why not by day?

"It is written: 'Today you are going out'; and, 'The One, your God, brought you out of Egypt by night.'[a]

"That night blazed fierce as summer noon.

"The Egyptians emerged from their houses.

"Their firstborn lay dead in the streets.

and Israel danced away before their eyes."[68]

Simeon did not say why the weak, the lambs, were slaughtered.

Moses declared before Pharaoh,

"There shall be a great cry throughout all the land,

but against any of the children of Israel

no dog shall move his tongue, that you may know how

the LORD puts a difference between the Egyptians and Israel."

Israel slaughtered the Passover sacrifice, splashed blood on their doorposts, and kept to their houses all night while the destroyer, who makes no distinctions, walked abroad.

Rabbi Eliezer the Elder warned the nations of the world:

"The holy One's vineyard is the House of Israel.

"Do not peep into it.

"If you peep in, then do not enter it.

"If you enter, do not breathe its fragrance.

"If you breathe the fragrance, do not eat its fruit.

"If you peep and enter, breathe the scent and eat the fruit, you will be uprooted from this world, and the next."

A midrash interprets a psalm's call to

"Praise the LORD, O you servants of the LORD"[b]

in light of the verse

---

a. Deuteronomy 16:1
b. Psalm 113:1

"I call to remembrance my song in the night;
I commune with my own heart."[a]
"Remember my song in the night" means Israel said to God,
"I remember the miracles You did for me in Egypt.
"I sang to you when you smote Egypt's first-born."
That's why the psalm says,
"Praise, O you servants of the LORD;"
not, "Praise, O you servants of Pharaoh."

When Israel went up from Egypt,
A house in a house of no law with strange language,
The land filled its promise to Jacob.
The sea saw the children on foot and drew back.
Jordan turned aside.
Boulders skipped down mountainsides like rams
Jump, like spring lambs.

What quailed the sea so it fled?
What shunted Jordan?
Skipped the mountainside?
The presence, God, which makes land pitch
Made rock melt into standing pools,
Cliffs spout fountains.[b]

---

a. Psalm 77:7
b. Psalm 114

WHEN HE SENT AWAY
STATES AN IMPOSSIBLE COMPARISON, WHICH IS IMPOSSIBLE TO SAY

BE-SHALLAḤ/בשלח—Exodus 13:17-17:16
And it came to pass, when Pharaoh sent away the people...
God led the people by way of the Red Sea wilderness.

When Israel crossed the Red Sea on Thursday morning, the last day of Passover,[69] Moses reassured the shaken multitude, "The LORD will battle for you."

And while God performed his miracles, the people asked, "What should we do?"

Moses told them:
"Exalt, acclaim, announce and magnify,
    give praise, song, glory and loud cheers
        to God, the One of war."

In that moment Israel sang:
"I will sing to the LORD, for He has triumphed gloriously..."
And the people feared the LORD.

In one legend, as the Israelites emerged from the Red Sea, the angels rushed in to sing before the One.

But God said, "Wait. Let my children go first. They are mortal.

"You, you live forever. You can always sing."

Rashi commented that people fear to sing God's praises, lest they say too little about more than can be said.

David the psalmist said, "Silence is praise to You."[a]

Rabbi Yoḥanan offered this comparison: "Silent like a statue. A thousand people look at it, and each one thinks, 'It is looking at me.' But the statue does not say, 'I am the LORD thy

---

a. Psalm 65:2

God, who spoke with you face-to-face.'"

Rabbi Ishmael emphasizes that Moses had to plead before he saw God's likeness, and even the Living Beings who bear God's Throne do not recognize the Presence. When it's time for them to sing they ask,

"Where is he?

"We know not here or there;

Wherever he may be,

Blessed be God's glory from his place."[a]

Eliezer the Great makes a further distinction. "God spoke through prophets in parables and appeared in visions, but at the Red Sea everyone, even a maidservant, saw things the prophets did not see and pointing a finger, said:

'This is my God, and I will glorify Him.'"

When Ishmael objected, "How can a human exalt the Creator?" Rabbi Yose the Galileian piped up: "I lift my voice

for pleasure and in praise of One who spoke

and the world came into being."

"Then sang Moses and the children of Israel this song

unto the LORD."

A midrash points out that this "Then" [אז/az] expresses joy, as in the Pilgrim Psalm:

"Then our mouth filled with laughter, our tongue with song."[b]

Even though God called to Adam in Eden, and was answered;

and Abraham served angels food and drink;

and Isaac asked, and God supplied the ram;

and Jacob dreamed and wrestled and prevailed;

none of them sang praise.

a. Ezekiel 3:12
b. Psalm 126:2

But Israel passed through the Sea and opened up their lips, and God said, "I've waited for this since the beginning."[70]

According to Rashi, when Moses saw the miracle, he was inspired, then he sang. The verb "sang" is written in Hebrew in the immediate tense [יָשִׁיר/yashir], which indicates both the present and the future. The orthography allows the rabbis to treat this as as an allusion to the resurrection of the dead in the world to come. "However," the elucidator argues, "the telling of this one-time-thing cannot be ruled by grammar, so the immediate, here, must be understood and translated as the past."[71]

Rabbi Abba thought that in this instance, in the Wilderness, the verb is suspended between the past miracle and the future redemption, when Moses and all Israel once again will sing this song.[72]

An expostulation of Simeon ben Yoḥai:
 Who is like you
in the world, in miracles performed by the reed sea?
 Who is like you
for your silent children, battered, when you hold your peace?
 Who is like you
among those who stand before you?
among those whom men call gods?
 You speak, and there is matter;
they have mouths but cannot speak.[a]
 You say ten things at once.
 You hear all prayers.
We fear for loved ones far away,

---

a. Psalm 115:5

but pray in fear when you draw near.
Others take their pleasure praising One who made the world,
    but my songs please the Maker.
I ask: Who like you, LORD, among the mighty?
He answers: Who like you, Israel, among the nations?[73]

    Jeremiah asked Jerusalem,
"To what might I liken you, for comfort?
    "Who can heal you?
Your prophets who spoke vain delusive visions?"[a]
Rabbi Joshua responded, "Compare Israel to the One
they praised at the Red Sea, singing,
    'Who is like you?'
    "He can heal you."[b]

    When the Rabbis wondered
"Who can heal your prophets for you?"[74]
    God answered through Isaiah:
"I have declared, and I have saved,
    I have caused to be heard;
You are My witnesses, I am God."[c]
    The son of Yoḥai took this to mean:
"Only when you are my witnesses, am I God.
    "When you do not witness, then
(How can I say this?)
        "I am not God."[75]

    Yose the Galileian drew a different analogy:
"Like the report that 'The LORD went before them

---

a. Lamentations 2:14
b. Lamentations 2:13
c. Isaiah 43:12

in a pillar of cloud by day,
and in a pillar of fire by night,'
were this not written in Scripture, it would be
impossible to say."[76]

JETHRO

HOW THE TEN COMMANDMENTS WERE GIVEN, AND HOW TO READ
BEFORE THE CONGREGATION

YITRO/יתרו—Exodus 18:1-20:23
Jethro, priest of Midian, Moses' father-in-law,
heard all that God had done for Moses,
and for Israel His people.

Once, an officer of the synagogue invited Rabbi Akiba to read from the Torah before the congregation, but he refused. When his students asked why, Akiba explained that he did not read because he had not prepared himself by going over the portion carefully, two or three times.

"A person may not read in public unless he has made the passage clear to himself," the Moses of his generation taught. "Even before the LORD gave the Torah to Israel, He first saw it and declared it, prepared it thoroughly and searched it out, and then He said something to man.[a] So, when God spoke all these words, He spoke first to himself, and then said them to Israel."[77]

At the foot of Mount Sinai, on Sabbath eve, the men and women stood in separate groups. God directed Moses first to ask the daughters of Israel if they wished to receive the Torah, and only then to ask the men, because (according to Rabbi Phinehas) it is the way of men to follow the women's opinion.[78] And they all replied as with one mouth,

"All that the LORD has spoken we will do."

Another rabbi maintains God remembered that, when He commanded Adam first, Eve strayed. "So," God reasoned, "if I do not call the women first, they will undo the Law."

---

a. Job 28:27-28

There were thunders and lightnings and a thick cloud upon
the mount, and the very loud sound of a horn. When the voice
of the horn grew louder and louder, Moses spoke, and God
answered him by a voice.

This shofar was the left horn of the ram caught in the
thicket on Mount Moriah when the voice called: "Abraham.
Abraham." Its right horn will be sounded in the time of the
Messiah.[79]

The master of the Zohar's learned company told them:
"The place from which the voice issues is called Shofar.

"There is no other greater voice, none more powerful.
"All depends on this voice,[a] a voice of sheer silence[b]—
      radiant, subtle, lucid."

What does such silence mean?

"Don't speak of it. Muzzle your mouth."[80]

A legend:[81]

When God gave the Torah
no bird chirped, no fowl flew, no ox mooed,
not one of Ezekiel's wheel-angels stirred a wing,
none of the seraphim said, "Holy, holy, holy!"

The sea did not roar, creatures did not speak—
the world fell silent. Then the voice went forth:
      "I am the LORD thy God, Who brought you forth
         out of Egypt, out of the house of bondage."

God gave all Ten Commandments in one utterance.

The Sages marvel: "Just as He takes life and gives life, He
afflicts and heals, creates light and darkness, makes peace and
evil,[82] He by whose word the world came into being can say

---

a. Deuteronomy 5:19
b. 1 Kings 19:12

two words in one utterance, a way of speaking impossible for human beings.

"There is none like Him, who spoke all these words. Humans cannot listen to even two people crying at the same time, but when all who ever come into this world cry out at once, He hears."[83]

In Maimonides' explication, Moses was spoken to and the people heard the great voice, but not articulated speech. It may be that all Israel heard one voice say the first two of the ten commandments at once, which Moses then made them hear again in his own words, each and every commandment as he heard it.

After they heard the first voice, the people were awed by terror, and said to Moses, "Why should we die? You—go near and hear.[a]"

Moses went up a second time and received the rest of the commandments, one by one. Meanwhile, Israel saw fires and heard voices and lightning, like thunder and the voice of the horn.

As for the voice from which God's speech was understood, Maimonides concludes the people heard it only once.[84]

The Sages said, "It had no echo."[85]

Simeon ben Yoḥai adds, "At that moment Israel saw eye-to-eye, and rejoiced; they and all later generations stood together, receiving the Torah at Mount Sinai."[86]

Tradition requires that the Torah scroll be read aloud by only one person, who must concentrate with all his heart and mind upon the words, for he is the agent of the Master's in conveying them to the people.

---

a. Deuteronomy 5:21-24

All must listen in silence, so they may hear the words from his mouth, just as if they were receiving the Torah at that moment at Sinai.

Another, a prompter or translator, should stand beside the reader, but keep silent, so that only one utterance is heard, not two.

The holy tongue is one, not two.[87]

Simeon ben Pazzi observed that, "when Moses spoke and God answered him, the holy One was the translator. Every word God spoke came out in seventy languages, so all the nations could understand. But when Moses spoke to Israel in the holy tongue, God had to translate for them.

"Or, one could say that Moses was the translator, and God took the place of the reader of Torah. Either way, neither voice was louder than the other."[88]

The school of Rabbi Nehuniah[89] taught that God gave the Torah and revealed himself through the Ten Sayings, in seven voices. All the people saw the voices.

King David celebrated what they heard in seven verses:

The voice draws longhand script on open water;
The voice helps gales halloo, stands waves on end;
The voice cracks cedar timbers hewn in Lebanon,
     skims boulders like flat stones thrown by boys;
The voice speaks fire, forks, its embers shake as meteors;
The voice springs tides, tears up the wilderness;
The voice drops forest leaves, makes mothers bear, leads
     animals to seek both heat and light come from within:
All sound less than a whisper of the voice which thunders
     underneath the backwash, in calm air.[a]

a. Psalm 29:3-9

JUDGMENTS

RESPONDING, HEARING AND DOING—
THE ORAL COMPARED TO THE WRITTEN

MISHPATIM/מ04שפטים—Exodus 21:1-24:18
Now these are the ordinances which you shall set before them.

Do I talk to the earth and the sky?
Did they answer?
"Days," they said. "Nights, they sung.
Wonder of wonders.
Liars believe that the world is their willing:
Dash them down
Now, Lord, like gravity's dancers. I drink
Understanding, and run off like water.[a]

First, God spoke the Commandments to Israel through Moses; later, the One wrote on two tables of stone.

Those present, all of Jacob's children, accepted the oral Torah without discussion and promised, "All that the LORD has spoken we will do."

They inhaled its meaning.

Then they exhaled.

The Babylonian Talmud[90] reports that as the people said "We will do" even before they said "We will hear," a heavenly voice asked, "Who has revealed to My children this secret of the attendant angels—first doing, then listening?"

In 16th-century Palestine, Moses Alshekh read "We will do" two ways: either the people believed in Moses' word and so spoke to the LORD directly when they said: "All that the LORD has spoken—according to Moses' word—we will do;" or, they meant: "Whatever we know to have been spoken by the holy

a. Psalm 119, "D"

One we will do—but not what you, Moses, have spoken."
Moses did not like the second interpretation.

Before he received the written Torah on Mount Sinai,
Moses wrote all the words of the LORD and built an altar. Then
he took the book of the covenant and read it aloud to the
people. Whether the Lawgiver taught from the "In the
Beginning" up to the giving of the Torah, as Rashi contends, or
he recited all five Books of Moses, as others claim, the people
answered his teaching with the words: "We will do and hear."

Maimonides notes that "to hear" sometimes means to hear
with the ear, and sometimes to accept. A Polish rabbi, David
Tevl Yaffe, paraphrased Israel's reply to their teacher as: "We
will hear in order to try to understand."[91]

It is one thing to accept the written word and its latent
meanings, another matter to say and do.

A medieval commentator thought that the people consented
only to the written Torah, not the oral, since they agreed to all
that the LORD has spoken, not to all that the LORD will speak.

In one legend, when Israel said, "We will hear and obey,"
God was not so sure of their obedience.

Israel claimed that heaven and earth would vouch for them,
but God said the Creation did not count.

When the sons of Jacob offered their forefathers as
guarantors, God objected that they were taken already.

So the people pledged their children; and God saw that as
good and sure enough.[92]

Another source maintains Israel accepted the written Torah
with all their heart, and all their soul, and all their might. But to
get them to accept the oral teaching, God had to hang the
smoking mountain over their assembled heads.

Moses left Israel at the foot of Sinai and went up to receive "tables of stone, and a law, and commandments which I [God] have written, so you may teach them."

Rabbi Levi equates "tables of stone"with the Ten Commandments; "a law" with the Books of Moses; "commandments" with the Mishnah,—the oral teaching; that "which I have written" with the Prophets and the Writings; and "so you may teach them" with the Gemara—what the students thought.[93]

In *Present at Sinai,* S. Y. Agnon further distinguishes between the two traditions: written Torah contains general rules, oral Torah, specifics; the oral is vast, the written, brief.

"And a cloud covered the mount."

In Yose the Galilean's chronology, the cloud hid Moses for six days. On the seventh day, God called to Moses from the midst of the cloud after the giving of the Ten Commandments. This began the forty days Moses spent on the mountain.[94]

The Zohar[95] identifies this cloud with the one shown to Noah, where God set his bow.[a]

Inside the mountain cloud, God's void and formless auditorium, writing, speech, thought and action are the same, like light before refraction. There, Moses walked the firmament. There, God gave Israel the Torah over strong angelic opposition.

In one account, the Creator rebuked the angels, saying, "If Israel does not receive the Torah, there will be no dwelling place in all creation for Me, much less for you."

In another story, Moses proved to a host of jealous angels that the Law was meant for humans, not for them. He asked:

---

a. Genesis 9:13

"Do you have many gods? Are your minds divided?

"Do you have a father or mother you must honor?

"Do you covet? Do you murder? Do you steal?"

In a third legend, God ordered Moses to seize the moment and set down the Ten Commandments,[a] because "right now the angels are confounded by my ordinance not to seethe a kid in its mother's milk. Take advantage of their confusion, and write."[96]

About confusion, Moses Maimonides observed, "No one ever questioned why the Law states God is one, or why we are forbidden to kill and to steal, or to exercise vengeance and retaliation, or why we are ordered to love one another.

"People argue about matters which do not seem useful, do not communicate an opinion, nor inculcate a noble quality, nor abolish reciprocal wrongdoing," the later Moses wrote, "like the judgment that prohibits seething a kid in its mother's milk."[97]

An old teaching:

One whose good works exceed his learning—
his learning will endure.

But one whose learning exceeds his works—
his learning will not endure.

For it is said: We will do, then we will understand.[98]

First spoken, then broken,
Then written and broken,
Then written and argued
        and pointed, not done.

---

a. Exodus 34:27

AN OFFERING

FINDS ROOM FOR THE INFINITE IN A FINITE WORLD

TERUMAH/תרומה—Exodus 25:1-27:19
The LORD spoke to Moses, saying:
Tell the children of Israel, to bring Me an offering;
from every man who gives from his heart
you shall accept My offering.

Rabbi Berekiah understood "Bring Me an offering" to mean:
"Lift Me up with your prayers."[99]
But when God then directed Moses to let them "make Me a
sanctuary, and I will dwell among them," the Lawgiver was
baffled.

As Rav Kahana tells it, Moses objected, "Not even the
heavens can contain You, yet You say, 'make Me a dwelling!'"

The holy One responded, "Moses, it is not as you think.
Though the tabernacle measures twenty boards by twenty
boards by eight boards on three sides, I shall go down to the
earth and shrink My presence, and meet with you there."

The four colors of the sanctuary on high were to be
repeated in Israel's tabernacle below.

Moses asked, "Master of the Universe, where on earth am I
to find these colors?"

God said, "Turn right. What do you see?"

Moses, "I see men wearing garments the color of the sea."

God said, "This is the blue which I require. Now turn left."

Moses turned and saw men wearing red.

God said, "This is the purple. Now turn back."

Moses looked back and saw a company wearing clothes of
blended red and green.

God said, "Make this color from the scarlet worm."

Then Moses faced front. Before him stood companies wearing white.

God said, "This color is fine twined linen."

According to Rabbi Tarfon, the Presence did not dwell among Israel until the people did some work.

Another says that God bade them make the Tabernacle because the people murmured against Moses. So long as Israel were busy with the work, they did not grumble.

When they finished, the One cried "Woe!"

The people said, "Maker of All, the work is done, and you cry 'Woe!'"

The Name replied, "I cry 'Woe!' for fear you will return to grumbling."[100]

Rabbi Simeon described the Tabernacle's inner structure: God commanded that the dwelling be modelled after the creation of heaven and earth, so the place below resembled the place above, joining them like body and soul.

Joined how?

Two cherubim, one male and one female, screened the arks' gold cover with spread wings. They cleaved in loving passion, just as in the beginning, God created heaven and earth, passionately cleaving.

On high, the cherubim stand with open wings, sheltering the ark. When the Presence comes, they beat their wings, lift higher, and sing from immensity of joy.

Likewise below, the cherubim in the Tabernacle stood and, at certain times every day, lifted their wings and spread them above the purging cover.

As Moses entered the Tabernacle, a voice descended from heaven towards the place between the cherubim. From there, it went forth and was heard by Moses in the tent of meeting.

Afterward, their wings again covered the ark.

When Israel were virtuous, the cherubim cleaved together, face-to-face. When Israel strayed, they turned away from one another.

Cherubim have a child's face.[101]

The master of the *Book of Splendor* exclaimed: "Cherubim! Children! Whoever remains among them, his face turns back into that of a child and he delights with them.

"Whoever is angry, bring him a child, and immediately anger subsides.

"Even though the Presence comes in judgment upon the world, once he settles upon the cherubim, he turns joyous, and the world turns back to compassion."[102]

A single cherub forms the living chariot of the visionary's God in Psalm 18, the One who "rode upon a cherub,"

His mouth a stadium
whose bleacher gates spat crowds of smoke and fire
streamed between tiered clouds,

Whose feet trod the black sky which came apart like
sea grass parts for horsemen at the gallop.

His wings were wind.

In Paradise, two cherubim guard Eden's gate with a flaming sword.[a]

In Solomon's temple, the holy of holies contained a pair of cherubim fashioned in olive wood plated with gold, each ten

---

a. Genesis 3:34

cubits high. Each wing measured five cubits. Two of the wings extended and met in the middle of the room to form the throne; two other wings extended to the walls of the tabernacle.

The Talmud records that, when the Presence descended, the cherubim stood and moved their wings on their own, lifting and lowering them three times every day.[103] As their wings beat and sheltered the cover of the ark, they chanted.

Ezekiel heard those beating wings.

In his vision by the River Chebar, the cherubim are four living creatures: each has four faces—lion, ox, eagle, man— each with the figure and hands of men, and calves' feet.

Each creature has four wings: two stretch up and meet above, to sustain the throne of the One; two wings stretch down to cover the creatures themselves.

The cherubim never turn but go straight forward, as do the wheels of the chariot. They are full of eyes like burning coals of fire.[a]

The inner walls of the temple in Ezekiel's New Jerusalem are, or will be, carved with alternating palm tree and cherubim. Each cherub has two faces—a lion's on one side, a man's on the other.[b]

In Moses' Tabernacle, cherubim also adorn the inner curtains and its veils. The curtains, woven with fine twined linen, and blue, and purple, and scarlet yarn, matched the colors of the Sanctuary on high. Each thread was spun out of four strands, one of linen and three of wool. These cherubim, Rashi explains, were woven into the curtains, rather than embroidered on. They were woven on both sides, with a lion on one side, and an eagle on the other.

---

a. Ezekiel 1:5-28, 9:3, 10:1-20, 11:22
b. Ezekiel 41:18-25

Rabbi Yose said, "Woe to the world, when one cherub turns away from his fellow, for look what is written:

'When they face each other, there is peace in the world.'"[104]

The Book of Legends records this proverb of a loving couple:

"When our love was strong, we could lie on the edge of a sword.

"Now it has grown weak, and a bed of sixty cubits is not wide enough."

Rabbi Huna inferred the same truth from Scripture: "In the beginning God said, 'There I will meet with you, and I will speak with you from above the Ark cover'—the Ark was nine handbreadths high, its cover one hands-breadth thick: ten handbreadths space in all.

"Later, the house King Solomon built for the LORD measured sixty cubits long, twenty cubits wide, and thirty cubits high.[a]

"But in the end the LORD said,

'The heaven is my throne, the earth my footstool.

'Where might you make a house for me?

'Where place my dwelling?'"[b]

---

a. 1Kings 6:2
b. Isaiah 66:1

YOU, CHARGE

ABOUT THE HIGH PRIEST'S BESPOKE WARDROBE

TETSAVVEH/תצוה—Exodus 27:20-30:10
And you, charge the children of Israel
to bring you pure beaten olive oil for light,
for a lamp that burns constantly.

Moses custom-ordered a breastplate, an ephod, and a robe, a broidered coat, a mitre, and a girdle, to dress the high priest. Despite his detailed instructions, no firm idea of the breastplate and ephod survives.

Rashi thought the breastplate [חֹשֶׁן/ḥoshen] was a jeweled ornament. He suspected that the אֵפוֹד/ephod tied across the high priest's back, much like an apron. Its left and right shoulder pieces were joined by woven straps across the ephod's top; an onyx stone was set in each shoulder. The names of the children of Israel were engraved on each onyx, six on one, six on the other, in the order of their birth. On the right shoulder-piece, Joseph (the sixth-born) was spelled Jehoseph, with an additional ה/he, so that both stones contained the same number of letters.[105]

The high priest's ephod differs from the linen item mentioned in Leviticus and in both books of Samuel. Aaron's ornate ceremonial outer garment featured dyed wool and gold thread as well as linen. Judges and Samuel[a] describe the ephod as an oracular alternative to prophetic inspiration. Elsewhere,[b] the ephod is a golden idol.[106]

The breastplate of judgment hung from the shoulder onyxes, and covered the high priest's heart.

---

a. Judges 18:5; 1Samuel 14:3-42, 22:18, 23:9-11, 30:7-8
b. Hosea 3:4

Fashioned from the same materials as Aaron's ephod, the breastplate was a square pouch set with four rows of three precious stones. The King James Version names the Hebrew gems: sardius, topaz, and carbuncle; emerald, sapphire, and diamond; ligure, agate and amethyst; beryl, onyx, and jasper. Other sources differ about their mineralogical identity.

Each precious stone was a seal engraved with the name of one of Jacob's twelve sons. Since the names of Israel's children lack the letters ח/ḥet and ט/tet, the twelve signets also bore the names of the three Patriarchs and the statement "All these the twelve tribes of Israel," to complete the alphabet.[107]

Some say the settings in stone, four rows of stones are chips of that stone the Creator threw into the abyss, where it stayed, and formed the world's foundation.

Rabbi Simeon added that the twelve stones served as Jacob's pillow, which he set up to be the house of God, the house of judgment.[108]

Rabbi Nehemiah[109] reasoned that the names of the twelve tribes could not have been written on the twelve gems in ink, because Scripture specified engravings of a signet; nor could a chisel be used to incise the letters, since Scripture required the stones must remain in their fullnesses.

To inscribe the gems for the shoulder pieces on the ephod and on the breastplate Moses' craftsmen called upon the *shamir*. An adamantine worm the size of a barley grain, the *shamir* was created at twilight on the first Sabbath, along with the tablets of the Law, the shape of the twenty-two letters, and the instrument that wrote them.[110]

First, they wrote lightly in ink on the stones' surface. Then the jewelers passed the *shamir* over the gems, and the traced letters emerged like gullies in spring rain.

Within the high priest's breastplate of judgment were the Urim and the Tummim.

According to the Zohar,[111] the Urim are the shining mirror. Embedded in its radiance is the Name formed by the first forty-two letters of the Torah, from "In the beginning" through "void." By that Name worlds were created.

The Tummim contain the same letters, embedded in the mirror that does not shine. This darkness absorbs the seventy-two-letter Holy Name concealed in the three, seventy-two letter verses that describe the parting of the Red Sea.[a]

Taken together, they are called Urim and Tummim.

Rashi deems Urim and Tummim [וְהַתֻּמִּים הָאוּרִים/ha-urim v'ha-tummim] to be that writing of the Divine Name placed inside the folds of the breastplate; by its means the high priest shed light [אוּר/or] upon and made perfect, completed [תמם/t'mam] his words.

Giambattista Vico imagined that divine names took shape when speech became articulate, through onomatopoeia. Thus, Latins called upon the roaring thunder—Iovis; the Greeks hailed the hiss of lightning—Zeus; the peoples of the East imitated the sound of burning fire and named their chief god Ur, whence came Urim, the power of fire.[112]

Beyond such speculations, of what matter and by what art Urim and Tummim were made, nothing is known.

In rabbinic tradition, the Urim and Tummim could be consulted only when the high priest wore both the ordinary tunic, pants, hat and belt, plus the breastplate, ephod, cloak and headplate. Even then, the oracle could be tried only on behalf of the king or a community leader.

---

a. Exodus 14:19-21

While the questioner faced the high priest, the Aaronite directed his attention toward the Urim and Tummim and the Ineffable Name written there.

As Rabbi Simeon tells it, once the high priest set the twelve stones in position and put them on with the breastplate and the ephod, the Presence would settle upon him. When the high priest inquired of the Urim and Tummim, the letters deep inside the stones which recorded the names of the twelve tribes would shine and spell out the answer.

The question was not put in a loud voice; neither was it asked inwardly.

"Be articulate," the rabbis counseled. "Don't ask two questions at the same time; after the first answer, ask a second question."

As oracle, the priest answered directly, without the words "God says."

Unlike prophetic speech, the judgment of the Urim and Tummim cannot be retracted.

Tradition holds that after the death of Samuel, David, and Solomon, the Urim and Tummim ceased responding. Rabbi Naḥman added that, even in the time of David, sometimes the Urim and Tummim answered the questions, and sometimes they gave no answer.[113]

In 1263, King Jaime the Conqueror of Aragon summoned the great Spanish rabbi Moses ben Nachman to Barcelona, to defend Judaism's position on the Messiah against accusations prosecuted by Pablo Christiani, a Jewish convert also known as Brother Paul.

The Catholic advocate argued that passages in Isaiah

concerning a rod coming forth out of the stem of Jesse[a] prove that, on the day the Temple was destroyed, the Messiah was born.

Furthermore, Brother Paul contended, Jews ought to be called Canaanites, since they adopted the Canaanite way of life and lived in Canaan. Christians, on the other hand, ought to be called Israel, since they have entered the place of the Jews.

Rabbi Moses responded that "one who takes the place of his brother ought to inherit his goods. If the Christians have taken our place, why have they not inherited our true goods, such as prophecy, and fire from Heaven, and the Urim and Tummim?

"Yet behold! we Jews, when we lost these things, have never found them in the hand of another; from this it can be seen that God intends to keep these things until we repent, and then he will return them to us."

To this, the convert had no answer.[114]

---

a. Isaiah 10:34, 11:1

WHEN YOU COUNT
LINKS DESIRE WITH TWO KINDS OF SONG

KI TISSA'/כי תשא—Exodus 30:11-34:35
The LORD spoke to Moses, saying:
When you take the sum of the children of Israel,
counting heads,
every man shall give a ransom for his soul to the LORD
when you number them,
so that no plague come upon them when you count.

The Zohar asks, "Why does a plague arise by counting?" and answers, "Because blessing does not dwell in counting."

At the end of their forty-day-long conversation, before sending the prophet back down the mountain to confront Israel's nakedness and shame, God put in Moses' hands two stone Tablets of testimony, written with the finger of God.

The shape of the written characters on the Tablets, the writing, and the Tablets were the last of the ten things created at twilight on Sabbath eve, on the sixth day of Creation.

Rabbi Eliezer records that, when Israel received the Commandments, they forgot their God after forty days.

They said to Aaron, "The Egyptians carried their god. They sang and chanted hymns before it, and saw their god before them. Make us a god like that of the Egyptians, and let us look upon it."

Aaron collected their gold earrings—the spoil of Egypt—and broke them into pieces. Some say he carved a mold; some say he put the gold in a bag and threw it into the fire.

Either way, out came this calf. And the people said,
"This is your God, O Israel,
who brought you up from the land of Egypt."

According to Simeon ben Yoḥai, two Egyptian sorcerers

were among the mixed multitude that accompanied Israel out of Egypt. These two, Yannes and Yimbres, were sons of Balaam. Balaam's father, Beor, is actually Laban, Rebekah's brother.

Magic, not art, made the golden calf.

When Moses descended the mountain, he was met by Joshua, who reported, "There is a voice of war in the camp."

Moses listened, and said:

"No voice exulting mastery;

no voice crying defeat;

voices singing I hear."

The King James version translates Moses' deliberations as, first, "the voice of them that shout for mastery;"

next, "the voice of them that cry for being overcome;"

and thirdly as "the noise of them that sing."

In these verses, Joshua uses one word for the sound that's heard: "voice" [קוֹל/qol].

In his response, Moses calls that voice, or shout, or cry, or noise that is or is not being made, "קוֹל עַנּוֹת/qol annot."

עַנּוֹת/annot, formed from the root עָנָה/anah, means "to sing or chant or utter tunefully." This verb also describes how, upon the Red Sea shore, when Miriam the prophetess took a timbrel in her hand and led all the women with timbrels and with dances, she sang or chanted for them (the King James reads "answered them"):

"Sing ye to the LORD, for he hath triumphed gloriously;

the horse and his rider hath he thrown into the sea."[a]

The imperative "Sing ye to the LORD," like Moses' prior song of triumph at the Red Sea,[b] invokes a different word for song: שִׁיר/shir. This Hebrew root makes both a noun and a verb,

a. Exodus 15:20-21

b. Exodus 15:1-18

and takes both a masculine and a feminine form. The feminine noun, שִׁירָה/shirah, specifically applies to Psalm 18, and to the two Songs of Moses, in Exodus and Deuteronomy.

What might be the difference between the Song of Moses and that of Miriam and the women with their timbrels, which are akin at least in name to the sound of worship around the golden calf?

One legend tells that when the holy One gave Moses the Tablets, they carried themselves. But, as he descended and approached the camp, heard the cymbals and dancing and saw the calf, the writing on the Tablets flew off, the Tablets grew heavy, and smashed themselves at the base of the mountain.

Rabbi Ḥiyya said: "Look at the face of the east, how it shines!

Now all those children of the east, of the mountains of light, bow to this light and worship it before the sun comes out.

For, once the sun comes out, many more worship the sun! But these people worship this first light, calling it

God of the shining pearl,

and they swear oaths by God of the shining pearl.

"Now you might say, 'This worship is in vain.'

But, since primeval days, by this light they have known wisdom."[115]

According to rabbinic sources, Israel worshipped the golden calf as an imitation of the bull in the Divine Chariot, as described by the prophet Ezekiel.

In his *New Science*, Giambattista Vico calls Minos of Crete "the first lawgiver of the gentile nations," the Minoans. In the *Odyssey*, Homer painted Minos as a just ruler, and one of three judges of the dead in the underworld.

Minos' mother, Europa, was carried off by Zeus disguised

as a bull. While King of Crete, Minos prayed to Poseidon for a sacrificial victim. The sea god sent a bull so magnificent, that the king could not bear to slay it. Minos' wife, Pasiphaë, fell in love and mated with the animal. Their union produced the Minotaur: a bull's head on a man's body. Minos confined the monster in a Labyrinth made by Daedalus, who was also held captive there, a prisoner inside his own creation.

Commenting on Moses' Song at the Red Sea, where "The enemy said, 'I will pursue, I will overtake;
    my lust shall be satisfied upon them,'"[a]
Rashi explains: "My lust [נֶפֶשׁ/nefesh] means 'my spirit, and my desire.'

"And do not wonder at a word that speaks for two words."

> We wait for you, God,
>   Even here.
> Choose someone of us,
>   Let him near
> You, brave enough to hear
>   Your answer.
> Winter gales spew oceans
>   Of salt rain.
> Mountain faces crumble, scree
>   Banks streams.
> Rivers muddied glide into the sea,
>   Mouths open.
> We hear the oceans inside
>   Seashells, see
> Whole cities in a puddle,
>   Taste the air.

---

a. Exodus 15:9

Your far stars blink in colors,
    Freak the jet.
A year breathes out and in.
    When rocks
Seem soft, the air has edges:
    All living
Shout your praises, or doubting
    Softly sing.[a]

---

a. Psalm 65

ASSEMBLED

A GUIDE TO THE PRACTICAL ARTS

VA-YAKHEL/ויקהל—Exodus 35:1-38:20
Moses assembled all the congregation
of the children of Israel, and said to them:
These, the things which the LORD has commanded,
you are to do.

Who has invented something out of nothing?
Spring days are hung on ladder rungs,
    And drying.
What once was tasted through the eyes,
Then later with the mouth,
    By nature,
Now must be done by cunning.

God's order for materials to be offered by the people, along with his detailed directions to Moses for making the dwelling, take two Sabbaths to be read before the congregation.[a]

The verses which record the accomplishment of the finished Tabernacle, Ark and all their furnishings, are the reading for a single Day of Rest.

Moses assembled Israel on the morning of the Day of Atonement.[116] The keepers of tradition emphasize that, in the entire Torah, only here does the text say, "Moses assembled."[117] Rashi further contends that "va-yakhel" should be translated "made to assemble," since Moses did not assemble the people with his hands, but rather caused them to assemble by his word.

In a Yemenite legend, the Sabbath objected to Moses' assembly:

"Master of the Universe! You created me on the Sixth Day,

a. Terumah and Tetsavveh: Exodus 25:1-28:43

116

and called me holy. Now you command Israel to make your dwelling without so much as a mention of my name.

"What if, in the joy of building, Israel should break me?"

God heard, and instructed Moses: "Write a verse about the seventh day before you start to build the Tabernacle, to make it clear that this work does not suspend the Sabbath."[118]

In just two hours, those assembled brought everything necessary for the portable sanctuary, with plenty to spare. One midrash comments that God blessed all they brought, so even little things were put to great use.[119]

The Torah does not spell out how the donated wood, gems, metals, hides, wool and linen were transformed into Tabernacle, Ark, utensils, furnishings and cloth. God entrusted the work to craftsmen endowed with wisdom of the heart. Their skill in practical matters can be understood as a manual tradition analogous to the oral Law which animates ethical and spiritual learning. This sensory wisdom informs the secrets of material creation handed down from master to apprentice.

The forty finished objects Moses required from the chosen artisans fill out a nine-verse-long list governed by a single verb: עָשָׂה/asah [to make or do]. Each item in the catalogue is marked by the accusative particle אֶת-/et, formed from the first and last letters of the Hebrew alphabet.

The word עָשָׂה/asah first appears in Genesis, on the fourth day of Creation, when God said,

"Let there be lights in the firmament,"

and "God made the two great lights—the stars also."

It is used again, on the sixth day, when God declared his intention to

"Make man in our image, and after our likeness."

In the second telling of Creation,[a]
"The LORD God formed man from the dust,
and blew into his nostrils the breath of life.
"And because He saw it was not good for the man to be alone,
the LORD God said: 'I will make a helpmate for him,'
and formed from the earth all living creatures.
Then the LORD caused the man to sleep, took one of his ribs,
and fashioned woman."
That is, God created things by saying, but male-female
humans and the living creatures He formed and made from
matter.

Rabbis Judah and Nehemiah debated which came first, the
light or the world. Judah favored light, while Nehemiah spoke
for the world.
Simeon the son of Naḥman, a master of Aggadah, argued
that, in a psalm, the Creator
"covered himself with light as with a garment,
and spread the heavens like a curtain."[b]
Therefore, Creation begins with light, as do workers in
material, who make things by daylight, or by lamp.

Genesis also supplies a genealogy of the practical arts:
Cain settled east of Eden, and built a city when his wife bore
Enoch. Tradition says God took Enoch living up to heaven.
Methuselah, Enoch's great-great grandson, fathered Lamech.
Lamech had two sons with his wife Adah: one, Jubal, was the
first musician. His other wife Zillah bore him Tubal-cain, "an
instructor of every artificer in brass and iron." No mother is
recorded for Lamech's first-begotten son, Noah, who followed

a. Genesis 2:7-22
b. Psalm 104:2

God's instructions, and made an ark.[a]

Noah's cursed son Ham had four sons.[b] Cush, the first-born, fathered Nimrod, founder and king of Babel. Nimrod's people spoke the language of Eve and Adam. Nothing restrained them from anything they began to do or might imagine and, using brick and slime, they built a tower to heaven to make a name.

Ham's second son, Mizraim, is Egypt.

Like the human image with respect to the divine, the Dwelling was the created world writ small.

When the LORD commanded Moses to build the Tabernacle, He nominated Bezalel to do the work.

God filled the master craftsman—whose name means "in God's shadow"—with that spirit which, in the beginning when darkness cloaked the face of the deep, moved upon the surface of the waters.

Besides wisdom, understanding, and knowledge of good and evil, God gave Bezalel the skill to teach and to do all the work—like the heavens and the earth when God finished them, and rested on the seventh day from all the work He had done.

The rabbis add, "Not Bezalel alone. God endowed all involved in the construction of his dwelling-place with good sense, intelligence, and ability. Even the cattle and beasts."

Bezalel asked Moses, "Where shall I begin?"

Moses replied, "My book describes the Tabernacle first, then the Ark. Follow the written order."

The sensible craftsman asked, "What is the purpose of this Tabernacle?"

The teacher answered, "It is a place for the Presence to

a. Genesis 4:17-6:16
b. Genesis 10:6-11

dwell, to teach the Law to Israel."

Bezalel objected, "Until the work is done, where will we keep the Torah? It is not fitting for the Light of All the World to be without a home. Let us make the Ark first, then the Tabernacle."[120]

And so they did.

But not on the Sabbath.

ACCOUNTS

ENOUGH!

PEKUDEI/פקודי—Exodus 38:21-40:38
These are the accounts of the Tabernacle,
drawn up at Moses' bidding.

The Book of Exodus is made of singularity and contradiction. A Hebrew raised by Pharaoh's daughter flees into the Wilderness, encounters a burning bush that speaks and is not consumed, leads Israel out of Egypt accompanied by signs and wonders through parted waters that swallow Egypt's army. The people eat food from the sky, drink water from the rocks, receive the Law, fashion an idol and build a dwelling for the Presence. From routine slavery, they step into uncertainty.

The book's work concludes with a numinous cloud, entered by an accountant.

Moses lacked confidence in his ability to follow instructions for making God's dwelling on earth, a thing which never existed before.

The Unpronounceable assured him that skilled artisans understand how things are made, and would know what is needed.

As for the Lawgiver's fear that the work would not be finished, the Creator answered:

"Do what I say; the work completes itself."

When Israel endowed the Golden Calf, they heaped up so many ornaments at Aaron's feet that they had to be told, "Enough."

Commanded to build the Tabernacle, they again gave so much material and gold that they were told, "Enough."

The holy One balanced the gold for the dwelling against

that for the idol: "When you made the Calf, you provoked me, saying, 'These be thy gods, O Israel.'

"But you have finished the Tabernacle with these accounts, and we are reconciled."[121]

Bezalel, the master craftsman, made all that the LORD commanded Moses. The artisan understood what God required for the dwelling, even details not specified by Moses.[122] Such knowledge is transmitted through the material, not by speech.

Judah Halevi regards the artist in light of skill and obedience: Every item Bezalel made—the ark, the lid, the carpets—was finished with the words, "Just as the LORD commanded Moses."

This "just" means, neither too much nor too little.[123]

When all the work was done just as commanded, Moses blessed the craftsmen:

"May it please God that the Presence dwell
in the work of your hands."[124]

Then he balanced the books.

Moses recorded all that had been done and all that had been made. Each entry finished that part of the work and set it in place.

Complete, the reckoning completed the dwelling.

And even though no blessing can dwell in anything that is counted, these accounts drew down the blessing.

Rabbinic chronology counts the seven-day Dedication of the Tabernacle from the twenty-third of Adar to the first of Nisan.

Every day, Moses erected the Tabernacle in the morning, brought sacrifices, then took it down. On the eighth day, he raised the Tabernacle and did not dismantle it. Some say that on the eighth day also, Moses took it down.

A Yemenite scholar[125] tells that on each of the seven days, as well as on the eighth, Moses set up the Tabernacle and took it down three times. That way, Aaron and his sons mastered the rites and the sacrifices, as well as the difference between that which exists entire and that which is composed from parts.

Kabbalists teach that artisans began the work, but the dwelling completed itself: Moses' accounts record that "All the work of the dwelling was completed."

Similarly, in Genesis, "The heavens and the earth were completed"[a]—the same verb, with this difference: that Moses' work was singular, God's many; or, that Moses's hands were many, God's one.

To the objection, that God "completed on the seventh day his work that he had made," tradition answers:

The world's works were finished one by one.

The whole was not fulfilled until the seventh day arrived.

With the Sabbath, creation completed itself.

All holy work completes itself.

When Moses erected the dwelling, all those wise-hearted artists wanted to assemble it themselves, but the tent would not stand until Moses set it up.

On the day the tabernacle was erected below, Moses could not enter because the cloud dwelt upon it.

The cloud was a single ray of the first light.

Rabbi Yose clarified, "This light, concealed and stored up for the world to come, has no role in this world, save on the first day."

Rabbi Judah added, "Had the first light not been concealed,

a. Genesis 2:1

the world could not have endured a single moment.
"Hidden, it is sown like seeds and fruit.
By it the world is sustained."[126]

Glory, according to Maimonides, is that created light God causes to descend in a particular place, as when the glory of the Name filled the Tabernacle. Glory is the essence of the One one shall not see, and live.

Viewed from the self, glory is how we honor the Name. All that is other than God honors him by apprehending His greatness.[127]

Isaiah declares "The whole earth is full of His glory,"[a] the whole earth bears witness to God's perfection. And full, like perfection, means complete, and coming to an end.

"From the beginning," Rav observed, "the Presence never had a home on earth. But when the Tabernacle was set up, the Presence dwelt below."[128]

Moses de Leon wondered, "Who spoke from the dwelling? When the Tabernacle was complete, the Ark spoke the verse:
'This is My resting place forever; here I will dwell,
for I desired it.'"[b]

Yose said, "All Israel chanted this psalm when the Temple was built and the Ark entered its place."

Ḥiyya offered, "The holy One sings this verse. When Israel performs His will, God turns from judgment to compassion, saying:
'Here will be my home, and when your children practice
My law, learn those lessons taught discerning hearts,
The poor shall have their bread, the wise know pleasure:
They will sing and dance and blow the horn.'"

---

a. Isaiah 6:3
b. Psalm 132:14

Which horn?

I lift up my arms, and watch the earth rise
Above its base self, upon pillars, on praise.
What lifts us up comes from within, without
One false note, or false steps, or deception.
Raise your own horn heads, brass with silvery valves,
Lift the bell full of blue sky and blow.[a]

a. Psalm 132

Leviticus

HE CALLED

AN ANATOMY OF BODY AND SOUL

VA-YIKRA '/ויקרא—Leviticus 1:1-5:26
The LORD called to Moses, and spoke to him
out of the Tent of Meeting, saying:
Speak to the children of Israel.

Rabbi Yose asked: "Why do we have young children begin their study with the Book of Leviticus? We should have them begin with Genesis."

The One replied: "As sacrifices are pure, so young children are pure; let the pure begin by studying things that are pure."[129]

Rabbi Judah and Yose studied at night.
Judah said: "Torah seems clearer at night than by day.
How can this be?"
Yose said: "The Oral Law explains the Written Law.
The spoken sways by night."
At night Job asked: "Now where is my Maker,
who gives songs in the night?"
The north wind blows at midnight.
It stirs the cock, who calls out loud: "You! Wake up, rise, gaze, breathe, and think on how we come and go and are."
They chant the Law, the one true song,
which dresses them in threads of dawn,
and makes them new, just like the day.

Simeon ben Azzai observed that, in the chapters on sacrifices, neither אֵל/el nor אֱלֹהִים/elohim is found. Only יְהוָה— the Name.

According to the School of Elijah, when the Temple stood, the morning sacrifice was offered for sins committed during the night; the evening sacrifice was offered for those committed during the day.

Another tradition reports that the altar took its sacrifices like a wolf takes its prey—one lamb at sunrise, one at dusk—and says of the offerings, that the ox is pursued by the lion, the sheep by the wolf, the goat by the leopard. So God instructed: "Bring Me an offering not from the pursuers, but from the pursued."[130]

In Hebrew, the word for offering or voluntary sacrifice, קָרְבָּן/qarban, has the same root [קרב/qrb] as the verb "to approach" or "to come near," the gerund "approaching," and the adjective "near."

Approach the altar. Make your offering,
　　and so draw near if not in space
(how to draw near to everywhere?)
　　then in, or at, that time.

Some say that, in the place whence Adam's dust was taken, there, in Jerusalem, the altar was built, citing "Then the LORD God formed man of the dust of the earth;"[a] and "An altar of earth thou shalt make for me."[b]

So long as the Temple stood, the altar within atoned for Israel's sins. Outside the Land, sages and their disciples still make amends for Israel, everywhere Israel dwells.[131]

In the second chapter of Genesis, the account of the generations of the heavens and the earth when they were created, יְהוָה אֱלֹהִים/adonai elohim [the LORD God] made man [הָאָדָם/ha-adam] from the dust [הָאֲדָמָה/ha-adamah], and breathed into his nostrils the breath of life [נִשְׁמַת חַיִּים/nishmat ḥayyim]; and man became [נֶפֶשׁ חַיָּה/nefesh ḥayah] a living soul.

In Genesis five, the book of the generations of Adam,

---

a. Genesis 2:7
b. Exodus 20:24

אֱלֹהִים/elohim [God] created them male and female, and He called their name Adam, in the day when they were created.

According to Rabbi Yehudah, when the One created man, he constructed him in a divine image, and breathed into him a holy spirit, comprised of three aspects: soul [נֶפֶשׁ/nefesh], spirit [רוּחַ/ruaḥ], and breath of life [נְשָׁמָה/neshamah].

The highest is breath of life, for she enables the soul to know and keep the commandments.[132]

Simeon ben Yoḥai said, "Not all humans are gifted with the breath of life. Some have spirit. Some only have an ordinary soul.

"Those who attain no higher than the ordinary soul cling to uncleanness, and see unclean things in dreams, some false, some true.

"A soul that's ready to receive the spirit's impulse seeks, and tries to rise, and learns what will occur both near and far.

"Joined with dust and soul, that spirit cleaves rock and mountain, ascending to a place among the holy messengers, where it learns many things before returning to its home.

The inspired soul can rise no higher until it gains the power to keep and know."[133]

In the beginning of Leviticus, Moses addresses "anyone" [אָדָם/adam] among the children of Israel wanting to make a voluntary burnt offering to the LORD from his herd, or flocks, or fowls.

The second chapter is directed to any soul who brings an offering of meal or milled grain.

The fourth chapter, concerning inadvertent, negligent, or ignorant offenses against the LORD, addresses "a soul" twice.

"A soul" is charged six times in chapter five, for sins of

omission and commission with ears, eyes, lips, or hand, against the LORD, and against another person.

According to Rabbi Menahem, Israel's lawgiver counts an offense against another person as more serious than one committed against the Creator. "It is written: If any one trespass, and sin through error in the holy things of the LORD, the offence is regarded as inadvertent. However,' Menachem warns, "if any one sin and trespass against the LORD by dealing falsely with his neighbor, the offender has committed a deliberate deception."[134]

Saadia Gaon, in his *Book of Beliefs and Opinions*, maintains that the soul and the body constitute one agent, and that they are rewarded or punished together.

"Some people," he observes, "believe that reward and punishment apply to the soul only, while others think they apply strictly to the body.

"Anyone who reads 'If any soul commit a trespass,' or 'The soul that sinneth, it shall die'[a] and thinks that sin and death concern the soul exclusively, is mistaken. When the Torah considers the guilt of a soul who touches any unclean thing, or of the soul that eats of that flesh, the expression soul can only refer to the body.

"Conversely, when Scripture says 'And it shall come to pass, that from one new moon to another, shall all flesh come to worship before me'[b] "and, 'let all flesh bless His holy name,'"[c] these bodily functions—speech and eloquence—pertain to the soul."

a. Ezekiel 18:4
b. Isaiah 66:23
c. Psalm 145:21

Like a mother bear her shapeless newborn,
Lick me into cub, O God–my proper shape:
I'd rather turn out true than clever, steeped
In arcane brews intent on power,
Wanting wisdom. Make me water
Melted from the summer glacier, run off
Over crushed bone, gravel, spilled
From the stone lip into singing pools.

The sound of water's better than the roar
Of animals burnt on an altar: the broken
Heartfelt not heart's blood makes sacrifice
Acceptable to God, which freshens Zion.[a]

a. Psalm 51

COMMAND

COMPARES DIRECT SPEECH AND WRITING, TORAH AND POETRY

TSAV/צו—Leviticus 6:1-8:36[a]
And the LORD spoke to Moses, saying:
Command Aaron and his sons:
This is the Law of the burnt offering.

The second part of Judah Halevi's *Argument for the Faith of Israel* closes with an extended discourse on the superiority of Biblical Hebrew, a language without a country.

The rabbi explains to the King of the Khazars that, "to pierce another's soul with an idea, direct speech is better than writing. There's even a proverb:

'From mouths of scholars, not the mouth of books.'

Our holy text is written with markings that take the place of those silences, intonations and physical gestures which shade meaning when we talk face-to-face. These cues tell the reader when to pause; they separate question from answer, prologue from exposition, distinguish haste from hesitation, command from request."

"Although it has degenerated and dwindled with its people, Hebrew is the language which God spoke to Adam and Eve, and they to each other. The speech of prophecy, teachings, songs and psalms, Hebrew rises and descends in David's prayers, in Job's laments and disputations, in Isaiah's addresses fitting present need to future hope. Moses, Joshua, David and Solomon did not want for the best word to describe strange matters and vanished objects—things we cannot easily articulate today," the exile Halevi observes, "because the language of Eden is lost to us."

---

a. Leviticus 6:8-8:36 KJV

Unlike the vernacular poetry of exile, such as Arabic that's written to an existing tune or in established measures, Hebrew verses are not governed by rhyme or meter. Each unvarying Hebrew trope may be sung to more than one melody. Torah passages with the same syntax are chanted to the same trope. Syntactical order, that is, meaning, measures the verse— something higher and more useful if less astonishing than poems formed in strict metric rhyme.

Poetry observes first the rules of artifice, rather than the direct exchange of thoughts. It is recited one way only, in the shape if not the sound of the poet's voice. "Poetry," the medieval Hebrew poet concludes in the rabbi's voice, "mostly connects when it should stop, and stops when it should go on.

"The Torah transcribes the living speech of others, a task unsuitable to poetry."

The king asked: "Why then do Jews long for a prosody in imitation of other peoples, that forces Hebrew into foreign meters?"

The rabbi answered: "We were, and are, perverse."[135]

In Babel, where the tower fell, strangers
    Do not speak our language. We were taken
There in chains and, captive by the rivers,
    Told to sing them songs of Zion. Crushed,
Could we sing Hebrew praises in translation?[a]

The School of Elijah taught that the verses commanding the meal offering, the guilt offering, and the peace offerings all begin with זֹאת/v'zot [and this]. The law of the burnt offering

---

a. Psalm 137

and rules for the sin offering[a] do not begin with "and." Sacrifices that begin "and this" can be repeated, and are favored by God.

Practically, this suggests that a man should not think, "No matter what vile thing I do, if I bring a burnt offering, God will regard me with favor."

Likewise, a person who says, "I will sin and repent, and sin again and repent," will be given no chance to repent.

God accepts the burnt- and sin offering only once.

On the other hand, no matter the number of one's sins, whoever feels guilt and offers up his soul in restitution, finds delight in this world, and prolongs his days in the world to come.[b]

As for peace, God told his children:

"Do good, bring sacrifices to be eaten by the givers.

"Offer the blood and holy parts on the altar, and I will rejoice."

"And," here, means: "forever."[136]

The Book of Priests refers repeatedly to the burnt offering, which burns upon the altar until morning. This repetition (even in translation) might be mistaken for rhyme, instead of the pulse of what John Milton termed a more solemn music, which consists only in apt numbers, fit quantity of syllables, and various sense drawn out from one verse to another, not "the jingling sound of like endings."[137]

For the unfit sacrifice and the fit, there is one law.

All that comes up on the altar shall not go down: the burnt offering; the meal offering which smokes upon the altar a sweet savor to the LORD; the sin offering; the consecration offering; the guilt offering; the peace offering.

---

a. "and this": Leviticus 6:7; 7:1; 7:11; no "and": 6:2; 6:18
b. Isaiah 53:10

Rabbi Simeon[138] concluded that
"The happy one looks up and says unspoken names;
    his fingers write small mysteries:
they rise out of the Wilderness like pillars, smoke.[a]"
    Yemenite sages timed their prayers to correspond with the
daily sacrifices, because a spoken offering refines and humbles
the soul, which emerges from confusion, and takes form.[139]

Asaph sang:
    God, God of gods
    (No other here pink morning peaks
    The violet quench of darkness falling
    Hiss into the sea) divided
    Portions at the family supper
        To some:
    I God am God I
    Need no roast lamb smoke
    In nostrils shifting guilt
    From sheep to goats,
    Enforced confessions.
    What I know you can't know,
    Would not tell you, were I hungry.
    I own all.
    Does God chew steak, drink goat blood?
    Praise, keep the law,
    And know not need.

        To others:
    Lip service, fingers
    Crossed behind your back,

---

a. Song of Songs 3:6

Thieves, cheaters,
False oath swearing tale bearers:
Am I dumb?
Is this my image?
I will smash your faces in
The mirror you make up to, gazing
Into shallow pools,
And there you'll sink.

Think, in time all will
Take the cup, and drink.[a]

Ezekiel wrote his vision of God's House in full sight of Israel,
complete with goings-out and comings-in, so that people might
keep the whole form and ordinances of worship.[b]

    Rabbi Samuel asked: "Was there a House of God then?"

    God answered: "When you concern yourselves with the
form, it is as though you build the House."[140]

What follows form?
    God told Israel:
"I accept what's offered of your own free will.
Reluctant sacrifice is made only for the fire.[c]
    You think I need your food?
The world is mine, and all its fullness.

"But even if I wanted food, I would not ask you for it."
    Why?
"I am merciful, and you are cruel.

a. Psalm 50
b. Ezekiel 43:11
c. Leviticus 22:7

"Blood dashed against the altar speaks to the blood you shed—
  Your need, and not my hunger—
  For you, not for me."[141]

EIGHTH
WHAT TO EAT, AND WHAT NOT

SHEMINI/שמיני—Leviticus 9:1-11:47
On the eighth day Moses called Aaron and his sons,
and the elders of Israel.

The Soferim, a band of scribes active from the Babylonian exile until the fall of the Second Temple, counted the number of letters and the number of words in the Five Books of Moses.

They found the middle words "sought to seek"[דָּרֹשׁ דָּרַשׁ/ darosh darash] in Leviticus 10:16 where, after the death of Aaron's sons, Moses was irked by the priests' apparent failure to follow divine direction to the letter. The Lawgiver sought to discover what had happened to the goat of the sin offering.

What letter stands at the very center of the Torah? Gimel— in the phrase "upon the belly" [עַל־גָּחוֹן/al-gahon]—also found in this portion, Leviticus 11:42, at the end of a list of creatures not to be eaten.[142]

A midrash[143] teaches that the first verse of the Torah portion for the eighth day begins with וַיְהִי/va'yihi [and it was] because on this day, Shemini Atzeret, there was joy in the presence of the One in Heaven, just as on the day the heavens and the earth were made by the word יְהִי/yihi [be], and it was.

This eighth day, then, is also the eighth day of Creation.

According to the *Seder Olam*, this eighth was the first day of the week, and the first of Nisan.

In one tradition, during all forty years in the Wilderness Moses wore white linen while he served as High Priest, and the Presence descended through him and dwelt in the world.

Another tradition maintains that, during the seven days' investiture of Aaron and the priests, the Presence did not descend through Moses. Only on the eighth day, when Aaron also began to serve as High Priest, did the presence come down to dwell in the world.[144] So, on the eighth day, Moses declared: "Today the LORD appears unto you."

On that day, Aaron's sons Nadab and Abihu also entered the priesthood, offered incense on their own authority, and were consumed by a fire from the LORD.

On his own, Moses could not understand four things:
how to compute the calendar, the new moons and years;
how to compound the anointing oil;
how to construct the candlestick for the Tabernacle; and,
which animals' flesh is permitted, which prohibited.
The calendar, the oil and the candlestick, God explicated step-by-step in Moses' presence. In the matter of the clean and unclean animals, God showed Moses one specimen of each, saying, "This you shall eat, and this you shall not eat."

In the first two of the last four verses of the Levite catalogue of permitted and forbidden edibles, the word "holy" appears four times. Twice the One commands:
"Be holy, for I am holy.... Because I am your God."

To make holy, Torah distinguishes between the pure and the impure, and divides living beings that may be eaten from living beings that may not be eaten.

Rabbi Abba understood the division to mean that "One who desires to have a share in life above, should guard his mouth from food and drink that defiles the soul, and from words of evil, so as not to be defiled by them."[145]

For the physician Maimonides, the "perfect Law" restrains desire. He wrote, "Most of the lusts and licentiousness of the multitude consist in an appetite for eating, drinking, and sex.

This destroys man's last perfection—the soul, and harms him also in his first perfection—the body. For when only desires are followed, as is done by the ignorant, the longing for speculation is abolished, the body is corrupted, and the man to whom this happens perishes before his natural term of life."[146]

Saadia Gaon wondered if perfection is found by dedicating oneself exclusively to holy service. Should one fast by day and arise at night to praise and glorify God, abandon all worldly cares, and believe that God will provide?

He thought not, and reasoned that if any person did not concern himself with food, his body could not exist. If a man begot no offspring, divine worship would cease with his generation.

"What chance," he argued further, "does the holy hermit have to comply with the rules of what is permitted and forbidden...? What opportunity does he have to abide by the laws of uncleanness and cleanliness?"

Saadia even ruled out allowing the aspirant saint to instruct others in the Law. "In that case," he concluded, "the service of God would be performed by those he instructed, and not by the saint."[147]

Until the eighth day of Creation, Adam's diet was confined to vegetables, and grain, and fruit. In *The Physiology of Taste*, J. A. Brillat-Savarin observes that "Adam was born hungry."

I, who do not keep the dietary laws,
am nonetheless relieved that I may not, need not eat
a camel (a "gimel" in Hebrew), badger, hare or swine,
    an eagle, ostrich, osprey, raven, owl,
       vulture, hawk, kite, cuckoo,
cormorant, swan, pelican, stork, heron, lapwing,

and others of their feather,
    much less bats.
I'm happy to keep cats and dogs,
    weasels, mice and tortoises,
        ferrets, lizards, moles and crocodiles—
all those abominations Brillat-Savarin calls "vermin"
    and Leviticus calls "whatsoever goes upon the belly"—
        off my plate.
Purity, like childhood and Eden, abides just out of reach in
Ezekiel's envisioned but as-yet-unseen New Jerusalem.
    Desire for perfection is not holy.
    Creation is, at present, incomplete.

And so, a toast:
    O God, the cup
    You pass to us
    Is crazed, is cracked.
    We drink it up.
        God said, On earth
    I'll rest my sandal.
    Jordan is my
    Fingerbowl,
    Zion's sky
    An empty doorway
    To my city.
        We said, But dip
    And we will sip, Lord.
    Always angry?
    Always praised.[a]

---

a. Psalm 60

SHE YIELDS SEED

THE RABBIS HOLD FORTH ON CONCEPTION, CHILDBIRTH, HOPE AND REGRET

TAZRIA'/תזריע—Leviticus 12:1-13:59
The LORD spoke to Moses, saying:
Speak to the children of Israel, saying:
If a woman be delivered, and bear a man-child,
then she shall be unclean seven days.

Aḥa, one of the Zohar's scholarly company, noted that the verse
"When a woman yields seed and bears a male"
skips over the nine months of pregnancy, and travels from conception to childbirth in one sentence.

Rabbi Yose chimed in, "True! From the day that a woman conceives, every day she gives birth! She can talk of nothing else, and hopes that it will be a boy."

"She Yields Seed" instructs a mother how to purify herself after childbirth:

Her male child is ritually clean after seven days, and is circumcised on the eighth day. The mother herself must separate from the congregation for another thirty-three days. After the lying-in period of forty days, she may return and have the priest make an atonement for her;

With a female, the infant's purification and the mother's lying-in are doubled: fourteen days for the child, and eighty days for her mother.

Leviticus defines differences: permitted and forbidden, pure and impure, holy and profane. It is a book of duties, not of hopes.

Maimonides explains that Biblical Hebrew has no word for the organs that distinguish the male or female sex. Neither are there words for the act itself. "There are things," the physician said, "about which one ought to be silent." Such modesty exists only in the sacred language. Common speech gives so many names, such graphic clarity, to the act of procreation, that what the Torah passes over still cannot be missed.

The eight-verse chapter on childbirth is the shortest in the Books of Moses. Here, the newborn is called not son, but זָכָר/ zachar [male]—the generic word for both humans and animals. In humans, it refers particularly to the circumcised organ. The only visible difference between a male and female newborn dwells in that little bit of flesh; its name derives from the same root as "remember" [זָכַר/zachar].

Likewise, the girl child is not called daughter. Rather, she is נְקֵבָה/niqevah [female], from the verb "to pierce." The word appears paired with male twice in Genesis: at the Creation; and in the generations of Adam: "male and female created He them."[a] In Ezekiel, female shares its root with נקב/neqeb—the setting of a gem, or a pipe.

In one commentary, God first made Adam as an hermaphrodite with two body-fronts, both facing outward. The Creator sliced the human apart to form two backs, one for the male and one for the female, who then turned face-to-face.[148]

Such is marriage.

"Think of it," Rabbi Levi said. "Human beings give a drop of fluid in privacy, and God openly returns it to them as complete and perfect children. While the embryo grows in the womb, the One shines a light by which the unborn sees from one end of the world to the other."

Hillel thought the female newborn is formed from the man's seed, and the male is fashioned from the woman's, like two artists, each reproducing a likeness of the other.

---

a. Genesis 1:27; 5:2

Of the fruits of union, Rabbi Simlai offers this account:
The nascent human embryo looks like the locust.

Its two eyes, nostrils and ears each resemble fly blow; its mouth looks like a barley-grain, its torso a lentil.

Its arms might be threads of crimson silk; the rest of its limbs are pressed together in a lump.

The female is dented lengthwise like a barley-grain.

Nothing outlines the hands and feet.

In the womb, the embryo is folded like a writing tablet: its head lies between its knees, its hands rest on its temples, its heels on its buttocks. Mouth closed, navel open, the unborn eats and drinks what its mother eats and drinks.[149]

Rabbi Abba tells another story about childbirth:
At the moment of conception, a spirit composed of male and female is aroused above. God entrusts the new-formed spirit to the angel appointed over human conception, and tells the angel where to place the spirit. Accompanied by its heavenly image, the spirit descends into this world.

First it passes through the earthly Eden where the righteous stand, row on row; then it passes through Hell where the wicked cry, "Woe!" and see no pity.

That divine image stands above the soul until it leaps into this world. In the world, all spirits emerge male-and-female.

After birth, their paths diverge. When a woman yields seed and bears, the soul must inhabit one sex or the other.

We live in this world, not in paradise.

Rabbi Simeon's son Eleazar disagreed with Abba: "How many millions come into the world? Yet from the day the Presence generates them, they are not souls until they settle in the body.

"For the seven days of the mother's impurity, the spirit roams her body to find its place. On the eighth day, the male soul joins to its body, and the child is circumcised. The next three days the child is in pain, and so the spirit does not settle in until the tenth day."[150]

And the female soul?

The old men do not ask, but it must be settled on the fifteenth day, when the mother ends her separation from the father.

Why does a woman bring an atonement sacrifice after childbirth?

Aren't children the blessing and seed of hope?

Rabbi Simeon explained the rite as reparation for an oath. "When she crouches to give birth," he said, "a woman swears she will never again embrace her husband. That is why the Law requires her to bring a sacrifice."

So why, if she gives birth to a boy is the woman clean after seven days, while with a girl she is clean after two weeks? The rabbi suggested that "when she bears a male all are happy, and the mother regrets her oath after seven days; but when she has a girl all are disappointed, and she only regrets her oath after two weeks."

All?

And why is circumcision performed on the eighth day, not the seventh? Simeon the son of Yoḥai explained that "on the seventh day the guests at the circumcision feast could not enjoy themselves, because the father and mother are still turned back-to-back."[151]

In this world, a woman bears in pain,
but in the world to come, Isaiah promises:
"Before her labor she gives birth;
instead of pain, she bears a man-child."[a]
Of the female-child, Ezekiel declares:
"You were in Eden, the garden of God,
where every precious stone bedecked you,
your well-wrought drums and pipes
set in you on the day you were created."[b]

Daughter,
If the matter's good, then manner hardly matters.
What's written in the heart a hand can copy quickly.
I love to look at you because no word escapes your lips
That was not written in your heart, and on your face.
So float majestically through life where others crawl:
Lies puff them up too large; truth keeps you small.
Because you love to do what's right, you deserve
The rare things: aloe soaps and lavender
Perfume, cedar closets full of skirts and dresses,
Silk shirts, buttons pearl and ivory, dainty
Speeches such as birds made Solomon.
Listen, child, you will leave home
Gladly, without tears, to walk with whom you please,
And everyone will want to meet your happiness.
Rich men's daughters and free spirits, true companions
Fill your grown-up house, and children, many more
Than met your father, who remembers that he loves
You, always, to himself, out loud.[c]

a. Isaiah 66:7
b. Ezekiel 28:13
c. Psalm 45

STRICKEN WITH LEPROSY

DERMATOLOGY AND THE TORAH OF DISGUSTING THINGS

METSORA'/מצרע—Leviticus 14:1-15:33
The LORD spoke to Moses, saying:
This shall be the law of the leper in the day of his cleansing:
he shall be brought to the priest.

מְצֹרָע/Metsora [one afflicted with leprosy] is a form of the noun צָרַעַת/tsaraat, and its passive verbal form צָרַע/tsara. Consistently translated as "leprosy," the word rarely appears outside Moses' books. There's the story of Naaman's leprosy cured by Elisha, of the four leprous men at the gates of Samaria, and the record of King Azariah's leprosy, and of King Uzziah's.[a]

Jacob Milgrom[152] has determined that the Hebrew Bible's leprosy is not modern medicine's Hansen's disease or elephantiasis. The Greek *Septuagint* translated "tsaraat" as "lepra," a general term used by Hippocrates for skin diseases resembling psoriasis and fungal infections. Leprosy, elephas, arrived in the Middle East when Alexander's conquering armies returned from the Indian subcontinent, centuries after the writing of Leviticus.

Nominal confusion began in the ninth century of the Common Era when an Arab physician, John of Damascus, called true leprosy lepra instead of elephas. In Andalusia, North Africa, and Mesopotamia, Arabic was the language of educated discourse. For Golden Age scholars and doctors such as Maimonides, tsaraat became leprosy.

Marvin Engel, a San Francisco Bay Area dermatologist, studied the biblical text and medical literature at Milgrom's request, and concluded that the symptoms described in Leviticus do not correspond to any known skin disease. Further,

a. 2Kings 5:3,6,7,27; 15:5; 2Chronicles 26:20-21

the problem lay not in the diagnosis, but in the treatment. Chronic skin diseases such as psoriasis, favus, and vitiligo, not to mention leprosy, do not disappear or even change within the week or two the chapter on cleansing assigns to the priest for diagnosis, quarantine, re-inspection, purification, and the offering of sacrifices for atonement.

Following Milgrom's research, Daniel Matt's translation of *The Zohar* calls metsora "scale affliction." In a footnote, Matt explains that the Sages understood the disease as punishment for evil speech, such as Miriam suffered when she spoke against Moses.[a] The rabbis repointed the vowels of the Hebrew affliction [המצורע/ha-metsora] and rebroke its syllables so that the letters read [המוציא רע/ha-motsi ra]—"the one who utters evil;" or, by extension, [המוציא שם רע/ha-motsi shem ra]—"the one who defames a person."

In *The Five Books of Moses*, Everett Fox chose to transliterate tsaraat, rather than translate the Damascene physician's error back into English, or replace it with some other uncertainty.

There are several kinds of scale affliction. Some can be declared clean after seven days. Others require a second week of quarantine. And some forms of tsaraat cast the person out forever.

The affliction, by whatever name, invites horror:
when the priest sees scaly eruption spread on bald scalp skin,
    that one is a leprous man, he is unclean;
the priest pronounces him unclean: his plague is on his head.
    The abhorrence runs both ways:
the leper's clothes shall be rent, his head shall be shaved,

---

a. Numbers 12:10

he shall cover his upper lip,
and he shall cry, "Unclean, unclean."
All the days disease is on him he is defiled;
unclean: he shall live alone; outside the camp he will dwell.

Accepting Torah means to hear and do;
sometimes "hear" comes first, and sometimes "do."
Remembering and understanding follow.

Rabbi Joshua the son of Levi said, "Torah' is used five times with reference to tsaraat.[a] Since metsora means 'one who speaks evil,' this five-fold repetition teaches that the slanderer transgresses all Five Books of the Law. That was why Moses warned Israel: 'This shall be the law of leprosy.'"[153]

The law for the afflicted one—who cannot hide his rash, his boils, his scales, his running sores, his inflamed skin from himself, from the priest, or from people in the street—also provides a path for the outcast back into the camp.

After seven or perhaps fourteen days, the priest visits the leper outside the camp. If he sees the affliction has healed, the priest must:

Take two live birds, cedar, scarlet yarn, and hyssop.

Kill one bird in an earthen vessel over living water.

Dip the red things and the live bird in the slain bird's blood over living (meaning "running") water.

Sprinkle the one afflicted seven times,

Declare him pure, and

Release the live bird into the open field.

Next, the purified one washes his clothes, shaves off all his hair, and washes in water.

a. Leviticus 13:59 and 14:2,32,54,57

Then he is clean.

After that, the outcast may return to the camp, but he must stay outside his tent another week.

On the seventh day, he again shaves all his hair, washes his clothes, and bathes in water.

On the eighth day, the now-clean person brings to the priest two he-lambs, a ewe lamb, flour, and oil to be offered to the LORD on his behalf as an atonement.

If he is poor, the penitent may substitute two turtledoves or pigeons, and the priest will provide a lamb.

The outcast leper is as good as dead, so the rites prescribed for scale affliction resemble the purification for a person contaminated by a corpse.[a] The ritual also parallels the consecration of priests in Leviticus 8, which transforms the everyday into the holy. But this purification transforms the living dead into a person once again acceptable to everyday life.

The ritual does not cure leprosy, but it does answer meaningless horror with a prescription to hold one's tongue. That remedies at least the disgusting things that come out of one's mouth, matters heard not seen.

Maimonides remarked that, given the many kinds of uncleanness, one can scarcely find a pure individual. The priestly restrictions serve to keep the sanctuary from becoming a place of common resort. For public health, "the belief that isolates the leper is obviously useful," Saladin's physician affirmed, "since leprosy is contagious and, almost by nature, everyone finds it disgusting."[154]

Or, as Satan answered the LORD, when asked a second time if he had considered the plain and upright Job, who held

---

a. Numbers 19:1-13

on to his integrity although God destroyed him without cause: "Skin for skin, yea, all that a man hath will he give for his life. But put forth thine hand now, and touch his bone and his flesh, and he will curse thee to thy face."[a]

When Rabbi Eleazar son of Simeon saw a leper,
  he hid himself[155] and wondered:
who knows or hears or thinks about meaning beyond words?
  A voice calls every day, yet no one listens.
  At dusk doors close, and out of the Abyss crawl
whispering marauders, while dreams blanket sleepers.
  Midnight a cool wind stirs; then the unspoken visits those
      who study in old Eden;
But most dream on until the cock crows dreamers out of bed.
  And so it goes.
Then on a day, the silent hand draws the afflicted back to dust,
  leaving others to offer up what lasts:
    a sacrifice of words, soul's only matter.[156]

So much for the Torah of disgusting things.

---

a. Job 2:4-5

AFTER THE DEATH
THE SECTION OF SEXUAL LICENTIOUSNESS, WITH GOATS AND EXCURSIONS
INTO THE HEART OF NATURE

ʾAḤAREI MOT/אחרי מות—Leviticus 16:1-18:30
The LORD spoke to Moses after the death of Aaron's two sons,
who approached the presence of the LORD, and died.

God opened his lecture with goats, and closed with bestiality.

Moses must instruct his brother Aaron the high priest in "the ordinances you shall do," which stand the test of reason, and spell out "those statutes you shall keep," which other nations call irrational. Of them God says,

"I am the LORD—

"I set them down.

"You may not question them."[157]

On the Day of Atonement, the Levite takes two goats for the sin-offering, sets them before the LORD, and casts lots upon the pair: one for the LORD, the other for Azazel.

Why two goats?

Ben Zoma explained that, on The Day of Atonement, we throw the angel of death a bone, because the world needs him—greedy dog that he is. While he toys with the bone, whoever wishes to may enter God's house unchallenged. And after it's done, the dog wags his tail.[158]

The Hebrew word for "goat" [שָׂעִיר/sa'ir] also means "satyr."

On the day the LORD wreaks vengeance on the nations, Isaiah warns, "The satyr shall cry to his fellow."[a]

For the Atonement offering, Moses specifies the two goats using this plural form: הַשְּׂעִירִם/ha-sirim. Here, and nowhere else.

---

a. Isaiah 34:14

Elsewhere in Scripture, ha-sirim means satyrs—
"In desolate Babylon where wild beasts of the desert shall lie,
   and owls dwell, and satyrs dance"[a]—
or it means demons, to whom the children of Israel shall no
more offer sacrifices, as Solomon's rebellious son Jeroboam
did when he set priests in the demons' high places over the
ten tribes of Israel.[b]

A fragment by Hesiod—Isaiah's near contemporary—records that
   The daughters of Hecaterus bore
      the lovely mountain nymphs,
      the tribe of worthless, helpless satyrs,
and the half-gods who reared Zeus, old dancing masters.[159]

   An Homeric Hymn[160] celebrates
Pan, the bearded son of Hermes with goat's feet and two horns,
   Lover of merry noise, who rules every hilltop and
      mountain peak.
   Days he hunts wild beasts among the slopes.
   Evenings he returns to woodland glades and plays
   notes sweet and low on his reed pipes.
   The clear-voiced nymphs dance with him then,
   and sing beside some darkened spring,
   while Echo wails on the mountain-top.

Giambattista Vico located the origins of Greek tragedy in
the satire (or satyr play) which accompanied the wine-grape
harvest. Peasant actors masked their feet, legs and thighs with
goat skins, painted their breasts and faces with vintage lees,
fitted horns to their foreheads, and hurled abuse at their betters.

a. Isaiah 13:21
b. 2Chronicles 11:15

Friedrich Nietzsche believed the orgiastic satyr chorus absorbed a civilized person "back into the heart of nature, where life is at bottom indestructibly joyful and powerful."

The Zohar treats Leviticus 18 as a separate portion, "The Section of Sexual Licentiousness" (or "Nakedness," or "Genitals"). Here, God cautions Israel: "Do not do after the doings of the land of Egypt, and of Canaan: I am the LORD your God," repeating "I am the LORD" a total of five times.

A midrash interprets this repetition as emphatic: The One who punished the generation of the Flood, and Sodom, and Egypt, will also punish those who imitate their strange ways.

The rabbis call Egypt's and Canaan's practices idolatry and adultery, but Rabbi Huna was more precise: the generation of the Flood were blotted out because they wrote songs to accompany rites for entering into sodomy.[161]

The prohibitions against nakedness sound like plot summaries for the Classical Greek tragedies, and a menu of panic dreams:

No one of you (both man and woman) shall approach to uncover the nakedness of their near kin, of:

your father;
your mother;
your father's wife;
your sister, the daughter of your father
or the daughter of your mother, born at home or abroad;
your son's daughter;
your daughter's daughter;
your father's wife's daughter;
your father's sister;
your mother's sister;
your father's brother;

your father's brother's wife;
your daughter-in-law;
your brother's wife;
a woman and her daughter,
her son's daughter or her daughter's daughter
(it is lewdness).

No one of you shall take a woman and her sister (at one time) to be rivals in their lifetime.

No one of you shall approach a woman in her period.

You shall not know your neighbor's wife upon your couch.

You shall not give your children to the priests of Moloch to pass through fire.

You shall not lie with a man as with a woman, or with any beast,

Nor shall a woman stand before a beast to couple:
This mixes and confuses human seed with animals.

A student of Elijah asked his master, "Which is worse: intercourse with a daughter, or with a daughter's daughter?"

Elijah replied, "Both are incest; here daughter and granddaughter are the same."

The questioner pressed on. "But the Torah does not say: 'Do not uncover the nakedness of thy daughter.'"

The prophet answered, "Son, if intercourse with those at one remove is forbidden, is not coming too near one's daughter even more so? Can't you draw a proper conclusion?"[162]

Rabbi Ḥiyya drew the line: "A man who lies with his sister, his father's daughter or his mother's daughter, and sees her nakedness and she sees his nakedness—they shall be cut off before the eyes of their people. It is חסד/ḥesed [a disgrace]."[a]

---

a. Leviticus 20:17

חֶסֶד/Ḥesed—"goodness" and "kindness"—also means "shame" and "reproach."

Rashi commented, "If you acknowledge that Cain married his sister, there God performed a kindness: to build the world from him.

"The world is built through kindness."[a]

After Cain killed Abel, Adam did not want to mate with Eve.

Rabbi Yose said, "Even before then. The moment they brought death into this world, Adam thought: 'Why should I breed for terror?' and separated from his wife.

"In those years, two female spirits came to him in his sleep, and coupled with Adam, engendering demons called 'Afflictions of the Children of the Earth,'[b] who to this day lure humans at doorways, wells and toilets.

"While Adam turned his back, the serpent penetrated Eve, who bore Cain, the father of the wicked, and of spirits and demons. So all spirits and demons are half-human, below, and half-angel, above."

Adam's daughters were such beauties that the sons of God took them for wives.[c] The fallen angel Azazel, for love of Tubal-cain's sister Na'amah, laid bare heaven's desires to the children of men.[d]

Na'amah, which means "lovely," still lives in the great sea. Aroused by men's dreams, she wells up from the waves at night and takes their lust, but not their seed. From male urges she conceives demons, who approach naked women in their sleep, impregnate them, and beget more demons.[163]

---

a. Psalm 89:3
b. 2Samuel 7:14
c. Genesis 6:2
d. 1Enoch 8-10

In the time to come, the nations' guardian angels will accuse
Israel:

"Maker of All, these and those both worshipped idols.
These committed incest, and those committed incest. These
shed blood, and those shed blood.

"Yet these are going down to Gehenna, while Jacob's
children will inherit. Does God play favorites?"

He will answer: "How can I not favor Israel,
   who offered all for love?"[a]

The nations will respond:
"Take our treasures, just forgive us."

God will rule:
"Trade everything you have
   to gain one verse of the Torah you rejected,
you will not be forgiven."[164]

A psalm proclaims that in the time to come,
   The LORD will loose the bonds.[b]

Some say this means that God then will permit a man to
sleep with his wife during her period.

Others contend that, when the Presence dwells forever in
Israel, sexual intercourse will be entirely forbidden.

Either way, death's bonds, and the world's, will come
undone.[165]

"You shall not uncover the nakedness of your brother's
wife" was spoken at the same time as its opposite:

"If brothers dwell together..."[c]

---

a. Song of Songs 8:7
b. Psalm 146:7
c. Deuteronomy 25:5

Different peoples, families at peace with one another are like
Oil poured atop the head that curls behind the ears and down
    the front of Aaron's beard to his robed ankles, are like
Dew on Hermon, beads rolled down the sides of Zion's
    mountains where, commanded, we chose good, and life.[a]

---

a. Psalm 133

BE HOLY

THE RABBI WHO NEVER LOOKED UPON HIS OWN CIRCUMCISION, AND EVERY MATTER HIDDEN IN THE HEART

KEDOSHIM/קדשים—Leviticus 19:1-20:27
And the LORD spoke to Moses, saying:
Speak to the whole congregation of the children of Israel,
and say to them:
Be holy, for holy am I the LORD your god.

Rabbi Naḥum was called "the holy of holies" because he never so much as looked upon the image on a coin. When Naḥum died, people covered the faces of statues with mats, so their master might not see after death what he did not look upon in life.

A student asked, "The dead can see?"

Simeon ben Laqish parried, "The only difference between the living and the righteous dead is the power of speech."

The Jews of Palestine addressed Judah ha-Nasi (the Prince) as "our holy Rabbi." After Antoninus Pius had himself circumcised, the Roman emperor asked Judah to examine the mohel's handiwork.

Our holy Rabbi replied: "I have never looked upon my own. And I should look at yours?"[166]

When first created, Adam was clad in radiant splendor. Eve was so beautiful that not even Adam could look upon her. After they ate from the forbidden tree their beauty dimmed, and the man could gaze upon his wife, and know her.

Abba believed one must not gaze upon the rainbow, which refracts the divine image. Do not even look at the priests' fingers when they spread their hands, because the glory of the Name settles there. Conversely, if it is forbidden to gaze at a holy place, looking upon an impure place is still more perilous. Do not turn to idols.[167]

Maimonides' son Rabbi Avraham noted that the guardians of tradition took "Do not turn to other gods" to mean "Do not remove God from your thoughts."[168] In practice, this suggests that a seeker should approach God using the rational soul. Engage constantly, like David, who did not worship money,

> altars, rites and idols people made to dazzle
> certain but not self believers.[a]

The rabbis say "Be Holy" was spoken before the whole assembly because it includes the Ten Commandments, and reiterates the most essential principles of the Torah.[169]

The School of Elijah regarded the repetitions of laws and precepts in the Books of Moses—as when God gives the Ten Commandments at Sinai[b] and when Moses repeats them in the Book of Admonitions[c]—as an instruction to obey these words, time and again.[170]

Rabbi Ḥiyya reeled out the repetition of the Ten Commandments in the Book of Priests as a woeful chain: if you steal, you will deal falsely, then lie, and end up swearing by the Name.

Ze'era understood "Do not take the Name in vain" to mean: "Do not assume that scriptural authority is the same as your own, unless you merit such respect."

Menaḥeman added that, when a person rushes to respond to his neighbors' questions in the Torah's name, before long he will run out of answers.

According to Abbahu, God said, "I am called holy. When

---

a. Psalm 16:8
b. Exodus 20:2-17
c. Deuteronomy 5:6-21

you speak words of Torah you may be holy, too.

"Take care. Unless you possess all those qualities I revealed through Moses,ᵃ you may want the authority."[171]

The eighteen-verse instruction "Be Holy" stands between the Section of Sexual Nakedness and the one-and-a-half chapters which restate the anti-abomination laws with their attendant punishments.

The Masoretes emphasize that holiness specifically pertains to keeping the commandments. Moses Maimonides clarifies that the consequent uncleanness refers to idolatry, incest, and shedding blood. Disobedience, breaking commandments governing action or opinion, dirt and filth, and touching or sharing a roof with certain impure things—these too are unclean.

However, the Talmud states, words of Torah do not become unclean.

Holy is the opposite of unclean.[172]

In Andalusia, Judah Halevi explained that "where there is no holiness, there is no possibility of spiritual impurity, which forbids an unclean person from approaching anything holy. Conversely, holiness limits contact with impure things. Most of these restrictions apply only when the Divine Presence is with us, which in our day is not the case."[173]

And the old men of the Talmud teach, "Be holy" means: "As He is gracious, be gracious;

as He is merciful, show mercy."[174]

The plain sense of Moses' direction "Rise before a gray head" was glossed by Rabbi Yose as "Stand for a learned scholar as

---

a. Exodus 34:6-7

you would before the Torah scroll."

Yose also heard the command as a warning:[175]
"Rise in the world before your hair turns gray;
No honor's due the old man grown incapable of doing wrong."

Tanḥuma bar Abba taught the etiquette, and upshot:
"Don't take the gray head's favorite place, or contradict him.

"Question an old person with reverence.

"Don't interrupt or snap at him.

"Whoever disrespects an old man will forget his learning; his life will be shortened while he sinks into poverty
 and dies like a dog in the gutter."[176]

In the *Book of Splendor*, the precept "Do not curse the deaf" refers to words uttered when the cursed one is not present, and cannot hear it.

Every spoken word ascends, as Rabbi Ḥiyya tells it, and evil speech flies up to the Dark Void, arousing uncounted powers against the speaker.

Not so a word of Torah. That matter rises to the high place, receives a holy crown, and splashes in the river gushing forth from Eden. Light wraps its speaker.

A student who reads the Law without knowing how, his word roams the world and does not find a place.

Yet, when an uninstructed lover of the Torah delves and babbles in the Book, his babbling ascends. The holy One delights in every word and plants them by the river, where they grow into great trees called willows of the stream.[177]

The Sages say that, on one day yet to come, God will roll the heavens together like a scroll,[a] the way a reader unrolls and rolls the Torah.[178]

---

a. Isaiah 34:4

As for here below, the One who made it will fold up the earth and spread it out again, like a robe.[a]

Another midrash speaks about "The Book of the Generations of Adam,"[b] which instructed Adam's descendants in all forms of craftsmanship. This includes the proper way to rule a parchment for the Torah, and how to write the holy scroll.

Ben Azzai said, "Well and good, this story of a book. Still, I hold with Akiba that 'Love thy neighbor' teaches more with less."[179]

Rashi remarked that, since it is impossible to know if another's intentions are good or evil, a person can escape punishment by saying, "I meant well." "But," the elucidator cautioned, "God knows your thoughts, and recognizes every matter hidden in the heart. So Moses wrote:

'You shall fear your God;' and
'Love your neighbor as yourself: I am the LORD.'"

---

a. Isaiah 51:6
b. Genesis 5:1

SAY

THE TORAH IS NOT A MANUAL OF CLEAR-CUT DECISIONS

'EMOR/אמר—Leviticus 21:1-24:23
The LORD said to Moses: Say to the priests,
the sons of Aaron, say to them:
None shall defile himself for any dead among his people.

Rabbi Yannai explained, "A verse declares: 'In purity, The LORD's words are silver tried in the open before all men, refined seven-times-seven times.'[a] This means, the Torah does not hand down clear-cut decisions.

"For every word God spoke to Moses, He gave forty-nine arguments that proved a thing clean, and forty-nine other arguments that proved it unclean.

"Confounded, Moses asked, 'How then to know the truth?'

"God replied, 'Follow the majority.'"[180]

After Joseph died, the Egyptians defiled the Israelites and their wives.[181]

Tradition records that Dan's grandson Bedijah was married to Shelomith, daughter of Dibri, and served as straw boss under Pharaoh's taskmasters.

One evening, an overseer visited Bedijah's house to order a work crew. The Israelite's wife stood in the doorway and when she smiled at him, the Egyptian thought: "She is mine." He sent Bedijah to collect field hands and, while the husband rounded up laborers, the taskmaster sported with the wife.

Returning next morning, Bedijah saw the Egyptian leave his house, and the overseer saw him see.

That day, the taskmaster drove the Israelites to "Work, work harder," and whipped the husband almost to death.

---

a. Psalm 12:7

Moses had grown up in Pharaoh's house. When he came upon the overseer beating the Israelite in the fields, Moses looked this way and that, saw there was no man, and smote the Egyptian.[a]

The rabbis differ about the meaning of "he saw there was no man."

Nehemiah says Moses saw there was none to stand up and utter the Name against the Egyptian, so he slew him.

Others hold that Moses saw no prospect of anything good coming from him or his children or his children's children to the end of all generations, so he smote the Egyptian.

"With the Name. Or with his fist," according to Rabbi Isaac.

"And trusted," Rabbi Levi adds, "that Israel would keep the matter secret."

Moses finishes four chapters devoted to laws governing priestly purity, prescribing the role of the community in sacrifices and festivals, keeping the eternal lamp lit and offering the Sabbath bread, with this short story:

The son of an Israelite woman whose father was an Egyptian went among the children of Israel, and brawled in the camp with a man of Israel.

The Israelite woman's son spat out the Name, and cursed.

Those present brought the blasphemer (his mothers name was Shelomith, daughter of Dibri, of the tribe of Dan) before Moses, and held him prisoner until judgment was made clear to them by the mouth of the LORD.

And the LORD spoke to Moses, saying: "Bring forth him that hath cursed outside the camp; and let all that heard him lay

a. Exodus 2:12

their hands upon his head, and let the whole congregation stone him."

It is said that the fight broke out because Shelomith's son tried to camp in the Wilderness with his mother's Danite family. Her tribe answered that Israel's tents were organized by fathers,[a] not "your mother."[182]

Rabbi Isaac asserts that Shelomith never smiled at Pharaoh's taskmaster, thought she was coupling in the dark with her husband, and that the certain Israelite man who fought her unnamed son was Shelomith's husband Bedijah.[183]

But most commentators maintain that after Moses slew the taskmaster, Bedijah separated from Shelomith and took another wife, who bore him a son. This other son was the Israelite man who brawled in the camp after calling Shelomith's son "You son of an Egyptian," whose father is identified by Rashi as the overseer killed by Moses.

Shelomith's unnamed son then reviled the Holy Name, which he had heard spoken from Sinai.

Rabbi Abba said, "This reviling also revealed his mother's name. Until now she was known only as an Israelite woman. But he made Shelomith's name, who bore and raised such a bastard, a curse."[184]

Rashi says, "She was named Shelomith because she babbled, 'Peace be with you, peace be with you, peace be with you all' to everyone and, saying 'Shalom with everyone, she grew corrupt."

Her son appealed his heritage in Moses' court. When he lost, he rose up and reviled God.[185]

Simeon ben Yoḥai taught: "The holy One made the duty of

---

a. Numbers 2:2

honoring one's father and mother equal to that due himself, fear of them equal to the fear of God, and a curse directed against one's parents the same as cursing God.

"It stands to reason. All three are equal partners in a human being."[186]

Rabbi Ishmael concurred. "Just as in regard to the Sabbath no distinction is made between a man and a woman or between a *tumtum* (from the Hebrew for 'hidden,' a person whose sex is unknown or in doubt) and a hermaphrodite, there is no difference between honoring one's parents and honoring the Maker.

God told Moses to speak to the children of Israel, saying: "Whosoever curses his God shall bear his sin. And he that reviles the name of the LORD, shall die the death; all the congregation will stone him with stones; stranger or native, one who reveals the Name, shall die the death."

Ishmael argued that saying "When he blasphemes the Name" excludes the case of someone who curses his mother and father, unless of course he curses them with the Tetragrammaton.[187]

The son of Yoḥai agreed that, although it might seem a person is liable for death by stoning even if he insulted God with a euphemism, the crime lies in cursing with the unpronounceable Name. If not by stoning, he nonetheless shall die by any means.

Simeon also interpreted the next verse, "A person who strikes anyone's soul mortally shall die the death," to mean, "He who kills even one shall die;" and added there are also times when "Love your fellow as yourself" means "Make the death quick."[188]

Certain sages wanted to exclude Ecclesiastes from the Writings—they thought King Solomon flirted with heresy.

"Was it right," they asked, "for the Preacher to tell a young man to walk in the ways of his heart and the sight of his eyes,[a] when Moses teaches the opposite?[b]

"Is there no restraint? No judge? No justice?"

But the Preacher capped his verse with "know that for all things God will bring you to judgment," so they agreed that David's son spoke well.[189]

Rabbi Levi concluded that," in days to come, whoever calls Jerusalem forsaken[c] will surely die, like one who curses with the Name."[190]

A commentary on the Song of Songs links the verses
"My beloved spoke and said to me: Rise up and come away,
　　for winter is past, the time of singing is come
　　and the voice of the turtle is heard in our land"[d]
to Amos, Micah, and Isaiah's prophecies against Jerusalem, when

"The place of study will become a bawdy house,
men will go from town to town but find no pity,
　　wisdom will putrefy, the fear of God will cease,
and truth will be abandoned."

Where does truth go?

To camps scattered through the wilderness, where children will insult their elders for rising early, while they sleep late.

---

a. Ecclesiastes 11:9
b. Numbers 15:39
c. Isaiah 62:2
d. Ecclesiastes 2:10-13

Yannai cautioned: "If you see one generation after another cursing and reviling, watch out for the coming of the Messiah."[191]

And after taunts, the blessing.[a]

Asaph sang, with instruments, that
    Israel once saw the law made visible,
Took heart, built God's house in Jerusalem.
Armies rained night fire on Zion's mountain.
    Terror took them in their sleep.
Sometimes love in sight of danger
    Makes an old man angry
    Wishing for the end of time,
A dry well deeper than the hate of strangers.[b]

a. Psalm 89:52
b. Psalm 76

ON THE MOUNTAIN
MISCONDUCT INVOLVING MONEY, AND SPEECH

BE-HAR/בהר—Leviticus 25:1-26:2
The LORD spoke to Moses on Mount Sinai, saying:
Speak to the children of Israel, and say to them:
When you come into the land which I give you,
the land shall keep a sabbath unto the LORD.

The Sabbaths, of Years and of the Land, offer release from bondage and debt, redemption for all, and rest to the earth itself.

Rashi points out that the year that follows seven Sabbaths of Years is called the Jubilee because the shofar is blown— יוֹבֵל/yoveil [Jubilee] means "horn."[192]

The rabbis of Palestine pondered, "Is a patched-up perforated horn fit to blow?"[193] Their sages agreed that, if the patch hinders the blowing, the shofar is unfit, but if the patch does not interfere, the horn is fit.

What of the player?

Akiba taught that a man with a blemish that makes him unfit for priestly service is still fit to blow the shofar on New Year's Day. He may also blow the horn that, on the Day of Atonement, proclaims the Jubilee. But the pierced ear of a Hebrew who chooses slavery over freedom makes him unfit.

Johannan ben Zakkai explained, "That ear, which heard 'I am the LORD thy God, who brought thee out of the house of bondage,'[a] yet elected to serve flesh and blood—that ear, which heard at the foot of Mount Sinai 'Thou shalt have no other Gods before me,' is now the ear of a slave who got a new, another master."

Rabbi Judah derives דְּרוֹר/deror [freedom] from כְּמִדַּיָּר/ kimdayar [dweller in a dwelling]—one who lives wherever he

---

a. Exodus 20:2

desires, not under the authority of others.[194]

Eleazar, son of ben Yoḥai, conflates freedom with a bird:[195]

"'Yes, the bird has found a house, and the swallow a nest
for herself, where she may lay her young.'[a]
Some birds of heaven nest outside. Others, like the swallow,
nest inside any man's house, without fear.

"The swallow's Hebrew name is דְּרוֹר/deror. Once it has
produced its young, the bird stays fifty days, then leaves the
nest and goes its way, as it is written: 'You shall hallow the
fiftieth year, and proclaim freedom in the land.'"

On the mountain, God twice commanded Israel:

"You shall not wrong one another."

The first statement prohibits misconduct involving money;
the second forbids wronging by word, by speech.

Rashi clarifies, "A person ought not provoke his fellow, nor
give bad counsel that harms the other and benefits himself.
And, should you ask, 'Who knows whether I intended evil?' the
verse continues: 'But you shall fear your God;

for I am the LORD your God.'"

Simeon ben Yoḥai believed the spoken wrong more
heinous than financial misconduct, because there is no fear of
God in money.

Samuel bar Nahmani added: "Money can be restored; but
what undoes a spoken word?"

When Onkelos translated the proverb "Death and life are in
the power of the tongue,"[b] he rendered "the tongue" into Greek
as "spoon-knife"—a sword, one end of which could serve as a
spoon: Death on one side, life on the other.

A midrash on Leviticus reasons that, since the verse about

---

a. Psalm 84:4
b. Proverbs 18:21

the poor man selling himself to you calls the poor man your brother, you should treat your servant in a brotherly way.

"Do not lord it over him, saying, 'Warm this cup,' or 'Cool this cup for me,' when you do not need it; or tell him, 'Keep hoeing this vine until I return,' if hoeing is unnecessary.

"Should you object, 'But I do need it,' the truth of what you say is buried in your heart. And Scripture says of any matter hidden in the heart: 'Thou shalt fear thy God.'"[196]

It's a bad idea to violate the sabbatical year. Midrash Tanḥuma spells out the consequences:

First, the transgressor will have to sell off his possessions, then his fields, his house, and auction off his daughter.

Should he still fail to repent, he will peddle door-to-door, then borrow at interest, miss his payments, and settle the debt by selling himself as a slave—not bound to a brother but enslaved to a stranger, and not a righteous stranger but an alien idolator—the slave to a servant of idols and images.

God concludes his instructions for redemption at the Jubilee with one negative and two positive commandments:

"Make no idols;" and,

"Keep My sabbaths; respect My sanctuary."

Rabbi Simeon turned the ban on idols into a song of caution:

> In case you think, "I'll make
> An image of my own, and worship it,"
> Remember that "You shall not make"
> An image of a man or woman;
> Nor carve an idol out of figured stones;
> Nor raise a post of any kind of wood.
> Make no sculpture of a fish,

Or bird that flies, or any beast
That lumbers, creeps or crawls;
No images of angels worlds above
Or lurkers in dark deeps, in waters
Underneath the earth: no water snakes
Or dolphins, scorpions or worms;
No picture of what's mirrored in the water:
Not sun nor moon nor stars nor planets,
No passing clouds seen when you raise your eyes.
Make no model of the earth,
Its mountains, rivers, plains or seas,
And carve no statue of the sky:
If you do, you'll make the world unfit for me,
And I will make the world unfit for you.[197]

BY MY STATUTES
REWARDS IN THIS LIFE AND IN THE WORLD TO COME
BE-ḤUKKOTAI/בחקתי—Leviticus 26:3-27:34
If you walk by My statutes, and My laws you keep and do.

The day before the Torah was given, Moses read the Book of
the Covenant aloud to the people.[a] He recounted God's
instructions to Adam, the commandments given to the Israelites
in Egypt and at Marah. "Then," Rabbi Ishmael elaborated,
"Moses read them the laws about sabbatical years and jubilees,
and the section of blessings and curses that closes, 'These are
the statutes and the laws.'

"'And Israel said: We accept all these.'"[198]

In the epic acrostic celebration of the Law that stands between
the Hallel[b] and the Songs of Ascent,[c] the psalmist sings
"I considered my ways,

and turned my feet toward Your testimonies."[d]
That is to say: "Ruler of the Universe! Every day I planned to
go some place or other, but my feet always brought me to the
house of study."

Rabbi Abba expounded, "The singer considered the
blessings and the curses. As Elijah explains it: 'Our blessings
traverse the alphabet in eleven verses, from "If you
walk" (which begins with א/aleph), through "Made you go
upright" (which ends with ת/tav).

"'The thirty cursing verses span only eight letters, from the
sixth letter, ו/vav, which opens "But if you do not hearken," to

---

a. Exodus 24:7
b. Psalms 111-118
c. Psalms 120-134
d. Psalm 119:59

the thirteenth, ם/mem, which closes "Their soul abhorred My statutes."[199]

"'Even better, in Deuteronomy[a] the fifty-four verses of curses start with ו/vav and end with ה/he—only two letters, side-by-side!'"

"And," Rabbi Abin smiled, "in reverse alphabetical order, which means: I will turn back your curses into blessings, if you walk in my statutes."

Eleazar commented, "The sword and the Book come in one wrapper. Observe what is written, and be delivered from the sword. If not, then not."

Another said, "If you keep the Torah, it is as if you had written the commandments; or as though you made yourselves."

Ḥiyya explained that a person must both read and do. "One who learns and does not mean to practice—better he had not been born."

Yoḥanan added, "Better that one smothered in his fetal caul, than he had lived to breathe the common air."[200]

In his chapter on "Reward and Punishment," Saadia Gaon agreed with the prophets that the reward for man's behavior is not meted out in this world, but in the hereafter.

The Babylonian philosopher noted that Scripture leaves little to the imagination regarding retribution in this world, since earthly rewards are distributed in despite of both reason and justice. On the other hand, Torah offers no details about blessings of the world to come, because their existence can be rationally deduced.

Likewise, when God told Adam "of the tree of knowledge

---

a. Deuteronomy 28:15-68

of good and evil you shall not eat"ᵃ—an irrational prohibition—
he did not include the common-sense injunctions against
murder, adultery, and stealing spoken later from Sinai.

"So," Saadia reasoned, "if the only rewards the righteous
can expect are those promised to the children of Israel, who
more than Moses deserved the blessings of rains in their season;
threshing overtaking vintage; peace in the land; being fruitful
and multiplying; and eating old store long kept?

"But Moses never entered the Land.

"Therefore, whatever one's share on earth, the greater part
of any person's reward is meted out in the world to come."

Following this logic, the philosopher acknowledged that
"since God-the-Just ordered the killing of the Midianite
children and the extermination of the entire generation of the
Deluge, and continually inflicts pain and even death on little
babies, I can only conclude that, after death, some other state
exists where innocents will find their suffering redeemed."[201]

Elijah taught: "God's code of conduct is not like ours."[202]

Searching Jerusalem, the Tishbite found a child with
swollen belly lying on a dungheap. The prophet asked the boy
if any of his family were alive.

"No, none," he answered.

Elijah offered, "If I give you words to help you stay alive,
will you learn them?"

"Yes."

"Say, 'Hear, O Israel, the LORD our God, the LORD is
one.'ᵇ"

The child shot back, "Hush. No one may speak the Name."ᶜ

---

a. Genesis 2:16
b. Deuteronomy 6:4
c. Amos 6:10

As the orphan looked down to kiss the amulet round his neck, his belly burst and the boy fell face down, fulfilling the curse: "I will cast your carcasses upon the carcasses of your idols."[203]

When the king of the Khazars remarked that other religions promise an afterlife richer than that of the Jews, Judah Halevi's rabbi countered that "those bounties come only after death.

"The Torah does not promise, 'Do this thing, and I will bring you to a paradise of gardens and pleasures after death.'

"It does say, 'You will be a nation to Me, and I will be your God, and I will lead you. Some of you will stand before Me, and some will rise up to the heavens.'

"The blessings that await us after death are revealed by our closeness to God, through prophecy and inspiration, and by God's attachment to His people in this life, in the here and now—not some remote hereafter."[204]

Jeremiah wondered, "What can I compare to you, Jerusalem? What might comfort Zion, ruined virgin, heaving like the sea?"[a]

The prophet-priest asked God, "And what about rejection, abhorrence, forsaking and forgetting?"

God answered, "Go ask Moses. He taught all prophets that, of those few left alive, 'their hearts will faint in the land of their enemies, the sound of a driven leaf shall chase them. You will perish among the nations, and the land of your enemies will eat you up.'

"I will not reject my people or abhor them."
God said nothing about forsaking and forgetting.

Instead, Isaiah proclaimed, "A day shall come to pass when a great horn will be blown, and they will come back

---

a. Lamentations 2:13

who were lost in Babylon."[a]
In Palestine, the rabbis answered Jeremiah on God's behalf:
"When I am reconciled to you, then
    I will walk among you, be your God,
    and you will be my people—
Then I will comfort you,
    I Myself will come and comfort you."[205]

Back in Egypt, Moses saw how men burden women, grown-ups put upon little ones, and youth saddle the aged. By his own lights, the Lawgiver adjusted each Israelite's share of responsibilities so all might be fairly borne.

God told Moses:
    When I sent Joseph down to Egypt
    (Strange tongues spoken there)
    I took his brothers off his shoulders,
    Saved him from the chore pots.
    When he called, I answered him with dreams.
    I answer you with thunder.
    Split rocks gush bitter water.[b]

"Since you have set to rights My people's duties, in the Wilderness you will teach them how to offer vows before the LORD.

"Scale the value of each man and woman, of every age and station. Tell them: 'If you present something of that value, it is the same as offering your soul before Me.'[206]

"By the soul's merits (not in money), I will save you and your children from the pit, the furnace mouth of Moloch,[c]
and prepare a table for you in the presence of your enemies."[207]

---

a. Isaiah 27:13
b. Psalm 81:6-8
c. Isaiah 30:33

Numbers

IN THE WILDERNESS

A PICTURE OF THE TWELVE TRIBES DURING THEIR WANDERINGS

BE-MIDBAR/במדבר—Numbers 1:1-4:20
The LORD spoke to Moses in the Wilderness of Sinai
in the Tent of Meeting,
on the first day of the second month in the second year
after they came out from the land of Egypt, saying:
Count the heads of all the people, the children of Israel.

The Sages taught that, at the giving of the Torah
the LORD descended upon the mountain in fire;[a]
the heavens, the clouds dropped water;[b]
and the LORD spoke to Moses in the Wilderness;"
which means that, like fire, water and wilderness, the words of
Torah are free to all; or, again, that anyone who is not open to
all, like the wilderness, cannot acquire wisdom or learning.

Israel were counted on ten occasions:[208]
when they went down to Egypt;
when they came out of Egypt;
after the Golden Calf;
twice in the Wilderness:
first by their standards, and then for the division of the Land;
twice in the days of Saul:
once counting with lambs, and once with pebbles;
by David, for an eighth time;
and again in the days of Ezra;
the tenth census belongs in the future, "when the flocks
shall again pass under the hand of him that counts them."[c]

---

a. Exodus 19:18
b. Judges 5:4
c. Deuteronomy 10:22; Exodus 12:37 and 30:12; Numbers 1 and 26; 1Samuel
15:4 and 11:8; 2Samuel 24:9; Ezra 2:64/Nehemiah 7:66; Jeremiah 33:13

Sun Tzu, the philosopher of conflict, said,
"Management of many is the same as management of few.
It is a matter of organization."[209]

While the people trekked the Wilderness for thirty-eight years,
a sign would appear in the cloud when it was time to move.
Moses would say, "Rise up, O LORD, and let Your enemies
be scattered."[a]
The cloud then moved, and all who had livestock loaded
their beasts with utensils; for those without pack animals, the
cloud carried the baggage.
Trumpets sounded, and Judah's prince and tribe set out
behind their turquoise blue banner with heraldic lion.
The other tribes followed—every man to his own standard,
according to the emblems, each banner the color of that tribe's
ephod stone, embroidered with insignia:
Reuben's ruby red flag, emblazoned with mandrakes;
Simeon's chrysolite green banner, a stitched picture of
Shechem;
Levi's unnumbered tribe's pennant of red onyx joined
white, black, and red fields, sewn with Urim and Tummim;
Issachar's sapphire banner, deep sky for the sun and moon;
Zebulon's opal streamer, white scud for a ship;
Dan's jacinth, blue ground for a serpent;
Gad's agate, a black-and-white field with pitched tents;
Naphtali's amethyst wine-red flag flew a hind;
Asher's beryl ensign, an olive-tree emblem on aquamarine;
Joseph's sons' onyx banner matched the darkness of Egypt
plus, on Ephraim's the form of a bullock, and on Manasseh's, a
wild ox;

---

a. Numbers 10:35

Benjamin's standard, jasper in many colors, bore the sign of a wolf.

Now and then, a finger of light beamed down through the clouds and pointed the way.

As Israel marched, the Ark preceded them, accompanied by barefoot Levites.

The sons of Kohath walked backward, so as not to turn their backs to the Ark.

Tongues of fire flicking between the Ark's staves, burned serpents and scorpions, and slew Israel's enemies.

When the cloud above the Tabernacle halted, so did the tribes.

First the Levites would set up the Tent of Meeting, then pitch camp in a hollow square about the Tabernacle, each family in its assigned place:

Moses, Aaron and his sons camped to the east; the sons of Merari, Gershon and Kohath circled the Tent.

The twelve tribes formed a second square, twelve-thousand cubits on each side around the encampment.[210]

Hitherto, God had talked to Moses from the burning bush, and in Midian, and in Egypt, and at Sinai. Now, in the Wilderness looking at the Tabernacle, the One thought to himself: "Modesty is a beautiful thing."

From then on He spoke in the Tent of Meeting.

The Sages marvelled: "Lucky Moses! Out of six-hundred-thousand people, not counting priests and Levites and elders, God spoke only with Moses."[211]

מִדְבָּר/Midbar [wilderness] also means "mouth as organ of speech."

In his chapter on self-mastery, Abraham son of Moses Maimonides advises using the imagination "to conjure up images that inspire longing for spiritual matters and enthusiasm about the commandments. Visualize, for example, the encampments of the Divine Presence, the Levites and the Israelites, the fire and cloud pillars, to bring them to life," until you feel that you, personally, are witnessing these scenes.

"When it comes to real knowledge," he concludes, "hearing about something is less convincing than seeing it, and the inward picture's authority lies somewhere between hearing and seeing."[212]

> Always returning to the promise, I remember
> Some few kept in mind what they had seen
> Of parted sea, of wasteland nurture, law.
> Wandering the wilderness, they cried out
> To God, to their confusion, and were heard.
> Their children founded places, and were fed.
>
> So later generations fill their mouths with praises:
> Proud minds humbled clang on dentless shells
> Of greed, of grief, of gorgeous meditations
> In the captive darkness, until, light gone,
> They thought that death was freedom.
>
> So later generations fill their mouths with praises:
> Prisoners of self, good taste, they found no food
> To like, and did not eat, and would have died
> Had they not eased the grip on their own throats
> And let slip bread and water past their lips.

So later generations fill their mouths with praises:
A sailor's business is the ocean. On his watch
He peered into the abyss: wind twisted masts
Like paper, breakers boiled yellow, rigging
Crackled with drowned souls. The compass spun.

So later generations fill their mouths with praises:
It's possible to die from too much skill,
And possible to live not knowing how
The storm blew, how merchant port was found.
It's possible to live and never once be calm.

So later generations fill their mouths with praises:
They sing in public and before their teachers,
How water turned the salt flats into orchards,
How people settled cities, planted vineyards,
Sowed grain in fields, covered grazing lands.

So the story keeps returning, of great armies
Lost in deserts, of the small made splendid,
Blessed with family and flocks, of the wicked
Choking on their empty language, hands clapping
Shut the mouth. Some parts return to mind.
A wise one sees things, and may understand them.[a]

a. Psalm 107

TAKE

ON JEALOUSY, MARRIAGE, AND SAYING "AMEN"

NASO'/נשׂא—Numbers 4:21-7:89
The LORD spoke to Moses saying:
Take the number of the sons of Gershon also,
by their fathers houses, by their families.

After Moses ceded authority to Joshua the Ephraimite, the son of Nun taught Israel. Even then, the people asked Moses to interpret for them.

Although he tried to explain the post-Mosaic teaching, the Lawgiver found he did not understand one word Joshua had spoken. And a heavenly voice commanded: "Learn from Joshua."

Stung, Moses faced the Name and cried: "Lord of the World! Until this moment I wished to live, but now I long to die.

"Better a hundred deaths than one jealousy."[213]

The Hebrew word for "ardor, zeal, jealousy" is a feminine noun, קִנְאָה/qinah. Its root derives from the color of a face suffused by deep emotion, and also refers to the jealousy of a husband, and to a jealous disposition. All these subjects, and the verb קָנָא/qana [to be jealous] are exercised in the fifth chapter of Numbers.

The jealous man knows no peace. His recourse entails priestly intervention, blasphemy, magic, blame, shame, and blight; or, as an alternative, the fugitive purity of Nazirites' vows. These paired ceremonies of intemperate despair and tempered hope separate the consecration of the tabernacle from the 88-verse catalogue of offerings the twelve tribes presented over twelve days to dedicate the altar.

Unrolled in the Book, then, if not laid bare in time, the teaching about jealousy and the instruction for devoted service to the LORD lead to the altar on the day Moses received revelation, the Giving of the Torah. The anniversary of that day is Shavuot, the Festival of Weeks.

So dark is the chapter concerning the jealous husband that, when he arrived in the world of souls, Moses called upon Elijah to explain it to him.

Elijah said to Moses, "Here is what's written: The spirit of jealousy may come upon him, and he is jealous of his wife, and she is defiled; or, the spirit of jealousy may come upon him, and he is jealous of his wife and she is not defiled.'

"Jealousy derives from both sides, the false and the true: when the false spirit accuses, he is jealous, and she is not defiled; when derived from the true side, he is jealous, and she is defiled.

"How can truth be found in a spirit of uncleanness?

"All have tasted from the Tree of Good and Evil.

"There is evil inclination in us all.

"A good wife arouses the Evil Inclination, makes it jealous, just as the serpent was aroused by Adam and the mother of all living. So he seduced her, and brought death into this world."[214]

And all we know.

Or think we know.

Or but suspect.

The adjectival form of קַנָּא/qanna [jealous] refers only to God, as in:

And God spake all these words, saying,
"I the LORD thy God am a jealous God;"[a] and,

---

a. Exodus 20:1-6 and Deuteronomy 5:9

"For thou shalt worship no other god:
for the LORD, whose name is Jealous, is a jealous God;"[a] or,
"For the LORD thy God is a consuming fire, a jealous God."[b]

A Yemenite midrash teaches that four motives befit God alone: vengeance, cunning, pride, and jealousy.[215]

These four impulses are not becoming in a human because they keep no law, cannot be bridled, are self-begetting, and they do not die.

The husband's accusation may be groundless.

The Sages considered whether this jealousy is prompted by a spirit of purity that brooks no immorality, or by a desire to torment his wife.

The school of Rabbi Ishmael taught: A man makes such an accusation to his wife only if he is taken by a spirit of impurity.

But Ashi reasoned otherwise. "It is a spirit of purity. While Ishmael thinks the husband's accusation is optional, Akiba regards it as the man's religious duty. So," Ashi concluded," the husband must be moved by a spirit of purity. If inspired by impurity, how could one contend that such an impulse is either an option or a religious duty?"[216]

Whatever the source of his impulse, a man taken by jealousy must bring his wife to the priest, together with an offering of barley meal unmixed with oil or frankincense— "An offering of jealousy, an offering of memorial, bringing iniquity to remembrance."

Maimonides noted that, unlike the sweet burnt offering, the sin offering's smoke is like the sin, detestable and abhorrent.[217]

The priest then follows an elaborate recipe to prepare the bitter water that causes the curse:

a. Exodus 34:14
b. Deuteronomy 4:24

Take an earthen vessel.

Fill with holy water, and mix in dust from the Tabernacle floor.

Write down and administer the oath and curse recorded in Numbers 5, verses 19 through 22.

Blot the letters of your written version (which includes the Tetragrammaton) in water, and add that blotting to the dust and water.

Take the jealousy offering from the woman's hand, wave it before the LORD, and burn it on the altar

Uncover the woman before the altar.

Serve the bitter water.

Swear and drink.

If the woman is guilty, then the water will enter into her, and become bitter, and she will be a curse among her people.

And if the woman be not defiled, then she shall be free.

Rabbi Ishmael said of this ordeal: "Great is peace, for the One allowed his Name, which is written in sanctity, to be erased by water, so that there might be peace between husband and wife."[218]

Akiba, who regarded the trial of jealousy as a religious duty, asked, "Since the laws only specify a man, how does one know they apply to a woman as well?"

Yose the Galilean answered, "It is written: 'When a man or a woman commits any sin that men commit.'

"Scripture equates a woman with a man for all the laws in the Torah."[219]

Abraham ben Judah di Boton taught[220] that the day of the Giving of the Torah was called שָׁבוּעוֹת/Shavu'ot not only because it marks the counting of the weeks, but also because it alludes to the verse in Exodus: שְׁבֻעַת/shevu'at [an oath] before the LORD shall decide between the two of them.[a]

"The Giving of the Torah," he continued, "was like a nuptial ceremony, where bride and groom swear that their love will last forever, unless he finds something obnoxious about her.[b]"[221]

That oath also appears in the trial of jealousy:
"Then the priest shall charge the woman with an oath of cursing, and the priest shall say unto the woman,
'The LORD make thee a curse and an oath among thy people.'"

The result of guilt will be:
"This water that causeth the curse shall go into thy bowels, to make thy belly to swell, and thy thigh to rot.

"And the woman shall say, 'Amen, amen.'"

"Amen" is said twelve times in Deuteronomy 27:15-26. Each "amen" there punctuates a curse, declaring "Cursed be the man": Twelve curses; twelve tribes.

The "Amen, and amen," by which the accused woman concludes the priestly oath of cursing, are the first amens spoken in the Torah.

That is, if the books of Moses are taken in order.

And remembering there is no before or after in Torah. Two "amens": one "male" and one "female created He them."[c]

Resh Laqish said, "Whoever responds 'Amen' with all his strength, the gates of Eden open for him."

In one telling, on judgment day the Name will hold a banquet for the souls in Paradise. God will sit on his throne at

a. Exodus 22:10
b. Deuteronomy 24:1
c. Genesis 1:27

the head of the long table, opposite David.

As the first cup is poured, the Maker will ask Abraham to recite the blessing over wine.

Abraham will say, "I, who offered up my only son, am not apt to bless the creator of the fruit of the vine."

God next turns to Isaac, who replies. "I asked my father where the ram was, when his knife was drawn. Try Jacob."

Jacob, too, will pass, declaring, "I prospered by deceit. And married sisters."

Then God will say, "Moses, you taught, now make the blessing."

Moses demurs. "I was not worthy to enter Canaan. Ask another."

At last God will come to David. "Take the cup and bless us, Israel's sweet singer."

Who answers: "Yes. Who else is worthy? I will bless the wine."

Then the One who set the table will read verses from the Torah, and David will recite a psalm.

Which?

One that closes the first four books of Psalms,[a] and finishes
    "Amen"—

to which both souls in Paradise and those who dwell below will answer with a loud
    "Amen."

---

a. Psalms 41, 72, 89, 106

WHEN YOU LIGHT

THE PROPHETIC SPIRIT, AND A WORD ABOUT THE WIVES
OF THOSE WHO BECOME INSPIRED

BE-HA'ALOTEKHA/בהעלתך—Numbers 8:1-12:16
And the LORD spoke to Moses, saying:
Speak to Aaron, and say to him:
When you light the lamps,
the seven lamps shall give light in front of the candlestick.

Israel asked: Why light up lamps before You, light of the world?

God answered: "Not for Me, but to raise yourself, the way My cloud and fire led you up through the Wilderness."[222]

There, it is told, the people patted manna into loaves which tasted like moist cakes sweet as breast milk and murmured: "Now our soul is dry, fed nothing but this manna every morning, every evening. Who shall feed us meat? In Egypt we ate fish free for the taking, sauced with pickles, melons, onions, leeks and garlic." (Manna tasted of every food but these, because they taint the milk of nursing women.)[223]

Moses asked God, "Have I conceived these children? Have I delivered them that You should say to me: 'Clutch them to your breast like a father bears a suckling child to the land you promised to their fathers?' I cannot take this people by myself."

According to Tanḥuma son of Abba,[224] the One replied, "I gave you spirit and intelligence to govern. I sought no other, so you might enjoy greatness alone.

"You want assistance? Tomorrow choose seventy elders of the tribes, bring them before Me, and I will put some of your spirit in them for that day, so you are not alone."

When two men, Eldad and Medad, remained in camp and prophesied, Moses' firstborn Gershon ran and told to Joshua, who said: "My lord Moses, make them cease.

"Throw the cares of the community on them—that will stop their prophesying."[225]

Moses answered: "Am I jealous of your knowledge? If only my sons were like you.[226]

"Would that all Israel were prophets."

Moses is a burning candle from which many lamps were lit,
Yet the light of the first flame did not diminish.[227]

As part of an extended dialogue on the fabric of revelation and ritual, narrative and prayer, the Jewish king of the Khazars describes thinking as "a story that we tell ourselves. But,:" said the king, "unlike the Torah's story, social speech cannot say two things at once. Sometimes a parable or poem may seem to mean in several senses, which then gives pause. Yet were a person able to speak this way, who could hear and then say back his meaning in one piece?"

His rabbi agreed, and likened the living to weak-eyed persons who cannot bear bright light. "At best," he said, "we imitate seers who lived before us. And like a person with sound eyes can only look at the sun from certain elevated places, at certain hours of the day, a human only may gaze by divine light in certain times and places. Those times are the hours of prayer, the places, those of prophecy.

"This also explains the rituals ordained in the Book of Numbers. God commanded the construction of the altar for burnt offerings, the Altar of Incense, and the candlestick. The burnt offerings fed the visible fire, while the Golden Altar was reserved for the invisible, finer fire. The candlestick bears the light of wisdom and inspiration."[228]

Simeon ben Yoḥai warned, "Woe to the person who says that the Torah just tells stories in ordinary words. Were that true, I could compose a Torah here and now from ordinary words better than anyone, better surely than governments and school books full of high-flown language.

"When God's messengers descend here from the place above, they put on the material of this world. This allows them to appear on earth, and lets our world endure their presence.

"Going from lesser things to greater: like angels, Torah is God's score and instrument by which He made the world.

"The Torah has a body: words. This body wears a cloak that's seen and heard: the Torah's story. Those who know how look not at the draped cloth, but at the body. Whoever thinks that story is the real Torah, may his spirit expire."[229]

Judah Halevi describes prophetic speech as an embodiment. Through sensible perceptions, prophets depict the Maker's greatness, power, lovingkindness, omniscience, life, eternity, government, and independence, how all depends on God, His unity, and holiness. A verbal figure in one instant reveals splendor wielding instruments of power—the up-raised hand, the naked sword, fire, wind, thunder, the lightning which obeys Him, the word gone forth to warn, to bring the news, and to foretell. Angels stand humbly before Him. He raises the lowly, abashes the mighty, extends His hand to the repentant.

The Andalusian poet believed love and fear come to the prophet naturally, and lodge in his heart his whole life, and that the inspired seer yearns to behold his vision again and again.[230] Even a single repetition was a great event for Solomon, to whom the LORD appeared a second time.[a]

In his introduction to the *Guide of the Perplexed*, Maimonides cautions the reader not to think that great secrets are fully and completely known to anyone. "Sometimes, truth

---

a. 1Kings 9:2

flashes before matter and habit again obscure it. For Moses of the beaming face, truth flashed incessantly and night appears as day. For others like the seventy elders, the lightning flashes once, the spirit rests upon them and they prophesy, and then no more."[231]

Rabbi Azariah interpreted this love-song's verse[a]—"You have loved righteousness and hated wickedness; therefore God, your God, has anointed you with the oil of gladness above your fellows"—as an allusion to Isaiah when he wrote[232]

"As I walked about in my house of study, I heard the voice of the LORD, saying, 'Who will go for us?

'I sent Amos, and Israel jeered, "Among the scattered children of men, the spirit chose to dwell in this deformed lump of leaden tongue?"

'I sent Micah, and they struck him on the cheek.

'Now, whom shall I send?'

"Isaiah said, 'Here am I. Send me.'

"God warned him, 'You will be shamed and beaten.'

"Isaiah wondered, 'Am I worthy?'

"God answered, 'You have loved your people as righteous, and hated to show them as wicked. Therefore I, God, your God, I have anointed you.

'Before now, every prophet prophesied through one who came before him: Elijah's spirit rested on Elisha; Moses' spirit inspired the seventy elders. But you will speak directly from My mouth with a double portion of My power, saying:

> Comfort ye, comfort ye;
>
> Awake, awake! (twice over);
>
> I even-I, and

---

a. Psalm 45:8/KJV 45:7

Rejoicing, I will rejoice.'"[a]

The Book of Legends records that, after the seventy elders were appointed, all Israel kindled lamps and rejoiced.

When Miriam saw the lamps, she asked Zipporah, "What does this mean?"

After Moses' wife explained, his sister said, "These wives must be happy to see their husbands gain authority."

And Zipporah replied, "The wives—alas for them."[233]

a. Isaiah 6:8; 6:5; 40:1; 51:9,17; 51:12; 61:10

SEND FOR YOURSELF
THE PITFALLS OF HUMAN INTELLIGENCE

SHELAḤ-LEKHA/שלח־לך—Numbers 13:1-15:41
The LORD spoke to Moses, saying:
Send, for yourself, men to scout the land of Canaan,
which I give to the children of Israel;
send one man from each father's tribe, each one a chief.

Solomon applied his heart to seek wisdom[a]—that is, the young king searched out strange lands he did not know, which God had promised him. He sat at the feet of teachers and expounders, and when the spirit rested on him, Solomon composed three books of writings which added to the words of Moses, and to the psalms of his father David.

Unlike a poet who may fail to complete an alphabet-acrostic poem if the letters resist him, Solomon's songs had letters left over, and numbered a thousand and five.[b] Beyond words, Solomon sought out wisdom in all things done under heaven: how to sweeten mustard or lupines, how to brew a hot drink of equal parts wine, water, and pepper.[234]

Walking on the way with Rabbi Abba, Yehudah wondered, "Since the Creator knew the human would do what was forbidden and so be bound to die, why did God create him? Study doesn't help, nor does ignorance. The end is the same."

Abba replied, "Some things are hidden in the Book, some are revealed. Secrets written without vowel points ought not be asked about, or spoken."

Yehudah said, "We should not question, or read Moses' books aloud?"

---

a. Ecclesiastes 1:13
b. 1Kings 3:5-12; 5:12

Abba responded, "On high, God occupies three worlds:
    a world unknown and unseen except by Him;
    a gate through which the One is known; and last,
    the place below, where angels live.
God is there and not there now, so when the angels want to see
and know Him, He stays concealed until all those living beings
ask:
    'Where is his place of glory?
    Blessed be his glory from his place.'[a]
It is the same with us, made in his image:
    we begin life in this world of separation, where one is,
and then is not;
    we pass to the place above through earthly Eden,
from where the other world is glimpsed and known;
    the highest world, secret and unknown, no eye has seen,
O God, but you.[b]"[235]

Before Moses died, he wondered if the trees that grew
across Jordan were like those in Eden's garden. He taught the
scouts, "Do not enter the land as thieves.

"If you are asked, 'What did you come for?' answer, 'Only
for five figs, five pomegranates, and a cluster of grapes.'

"Asked, 'Do you intend to fell our sacred trees?' say, 'No.'

"Enter as emissaries, and come forth as peddlers bearing
fruit on donkey-back."

In Hebron, three giant sons of Anak met the spies. One
shouted, and the twelve Israelites fainted.

Two giants fanned the Hebrews and rubbed their noses
until they came to. Revived, the twelve said that they had not
come to destroy the giants' groves or idols, and the sons of

a. Ezekiel 3:12
b. Isaiah 64:3/KJV 64:4

Anak let them go in peace.[236]

In the Valley of Eshcol, the scouts cut a branch with one cluster of grapes, and carried it between two poles. By Rashi's reckoning, eight men carried one cluster of grapes, one carried a fig, and one a pomegranate. Joshua and Caleb did not carry anything.

Moses sent out his scouts on the 28th of Sivan, in the days of the ripening of early grapes. They returned forty days later, at evening, on the Ninth of Av.[237] The Lawgiver assembled all twelve tribes to hear them report. He hoped the spies had acquired a branch of the Tree of Life in Canaan, but they bore only fruit plucked from the Tree of Knowledge.[238]

They announced, "The land surely flows with milk and honey. Its fruit is strange, its peoples, strange, so tall, they seem to wear the sun like a necklace.... ('Huge, like Goliath,'[a] Rashi noted, 'six cubits and a span.')

"We were like grasshoppers in our own sight; and so were we in their sight."

And all the congregation lifted up their voice, and wept.

God said, "Today they cry for nothing, but I now save this day for when my people mourn their loss, in times to come."

Mesharshiya maintained, "The spies lied. 'We looked like grasshoppers to ourselves'—fair enough.

"But, 'So we looked to them?'

"How could they know what others saw?"

The rabbis countered, "In every place the spies visited, prominent people died; this kept the inhabitants busy with funerals, and no one asked about the strangers among them.

"When mourners gathered in a cedar grove to eat their

---

a. 1Samuel 17:4

funeral meal, the spies climbed into the trees. Looking up, the mourners said: 'Those people in the trees look like grasshoppers.'

   "So the spies didn't lie."[239]

An Egyptian letter written towards the end of the thirteenth century B.C.E. by the royal official Hori to the scribe Amen-em-Opet describes what a mission to Phoenicia and adjacent territories may entail.

   The senior bureaucrat instructs the scribe:

You have not gone to the region of the Hittites with the bowmen of the army, nor have you trodden the road darkened by day and overgrown with cypress, oaks and cedars reaching the heavens.

   Lions outnumber leopards and bears there, and Bedouin surround the roadsides.

   On the way south to Acre, where is the mountain of Shechem?

   The stream of Jordan, how is it crossed?

   Tell me how to pass Megiddo, which is above it.

   The narrow valley is dangerous: Bedouin hide under the bushes. Some measure four or five cubits from their noses to the heel (seven- to nine-feet tall) and are fierce of face. Their hearts are not mild, and they do not listen to wheedling.[240]

The School of Elijah relates that God and Moses conversed before the spies entered the Land.

   Moses asked, "Master of All, how do you judge the earth's inhabitants and the world you have created?"

   God answered, "With slowness to anger."

   Moses said, "How is that? People live well in this place, enjoy its fruit, and then rebel amid the plenty."

The holy One said nothing.

Later, when the spies returned and spoke ill and the people wept, God snapped, "They still don't listen?

"My wrath will burn their bodies.

"My angels who protect them will turn away as I shut up their souls in dark chambers, cast forth their bodies in the Wilderness, and smite them with plagues and destroy them."

Moses pleaded, "Don't. Don't let the nations say about you: 'Canaan's gods are mightier than those of Egypt. The LORD could not feed his children, and brought them out to kill them in the Wilderness.'"[241]

God said, "So Moses, now you require my compassion?"

Moses allowed, "Indeed, I do.[242] Before you took the seed from which you make man on earth, was I the one who set their ways?

"Let your mercy keep us now and to the end.

For unless you have mercy, who ever would be born?"[243]

KORAH

THE PIT THAT SWALLOWED KORAH'S COMPANY

KORAḤ/קרח—Numbers 16:1—18:32
Now Korah, the son of Izhar, the son of Kohath, the son of Levi,
with Dathan and Abiram and On, sons of Reuben, took men;
and they rose up before Moses.

Scripture does not say Korah contended, or assembled, or
spoke, or commanded, but "Korah took."
What did he take?
Nothing.
His heart carried him away.

Korah the chief Levite contended that Moses had written
the Torah's laws and ordinances on his own. He pleaded with
the congregation, "Do I work to obtain greatness only for
myself?

"Every one of us deserves high office, yet my cousin
Moses takes the kingship, and gives his brother the High
Priesthood."

Korah marched with two-hundred fifty disaffected princes
of Israel to confront Moses and Aaron outside the Tent of
Meeting. This crowd of would-be kings and priests clamored,
"We all are holy. Yet you sons of Amram claim the highest
offices yourselves. Your yoke is heavier than Pharaoh's."

Moses answered, "Other nations have numerous gods, each
with their own rites and many priests. Those peoples do not
worship gathered in one place.

"Israel has one God, one Torah, one code of laws, one altar,
one High Priest.

"You all want to be High Priest? Tomorrow, light your
censers and bring them before the LORD. But only one among

you shall emerge alive.'"

Then Moses fell upon his face and said to God, "If Korah and his company die any ordinary death, I will say: 'The LORD has not sent me, and your Law is my invention.'"

At dusk on the sixth day of Creation, God already had prepared the mouth in the earth that swallowed Korah and his house alive.

As Rabbi Judah told it, wherever a follower of Korah happened to be at the time, there the earth's mouth yawned and gulped.

"No," said Nehemiah, "the earth formed a funnel and, no matter where a rebel stood, he rolled into the pit along with all his substance."

Others sages added, "Not just money. Their clothes and laundry were consumed. Even a borrowed needle."[244]

Berekiah commented, "Strife is grief. The Heavenly Court inflicts penalties only on those aged twenty years and older; earthly justice punishes those over thirteen; but in Korah's strife day-old babies were burned and swallowed up in the abyss. Even their names were taken."

The entire congregation gathered outside the entrance to the tabernacle while the rebel faction offered incense. Korah's three musician sons stood with their feet in the earth's mouth, ringed by fire from the altar, and words died in their throats.

Overflowing, their hearts[a] cried out, "Help us, Moses."

God heard that prayer, and said, "They shall be saved. I want repentance. Nothing else."[245]

So Korah's sons did not die.[b] The Name raised a pillar from the deep for each of them, where they sit, singing:[246]

a. Psalm 45:2
b. Numbers 26:11

"The earth is hollow, and has jaws.
Mountains topple whole into the ocean
    Heart, which boils, bubbles."[a]

Torah even names the sons of Korah, once, in a genealogy: Assir, Elkanah and Abiasaph.[b]

First Chronicles[c] lists the three as sons of Kohath in the family tree of Levites appointed by David to tend the tabernacle and sing before the Presence.

Heman, the king's seer when David moved the Ark into Jerusalem, is identified as a descendant of Abiasaph. The same passage traces Elkanah's posterity through the prophet Samuel.

Throughout the psalms associated with the sons of Korah,[d] the singer prays:

Why lose heart?
Hear bottom now?
Remember how dank rumbles
Guttered through the deep?
    O my rock,
Can a rock be forgetting?
Is this night without starlight
Death in my bones?
    Where is God? Do you sleep?
What good is kindness to the pit,
Or accuracy in oblivion?
Silence comes before and after,
In the empty space around us,
    And is with us.

---

a. Psalm 46:1-3
b. Exodus 6:24
c. 1Chronicles 6:22-38
d. Psalms 42, 44-49, 84, 85, 87 88

Tradition teaches that the heart also overflows in prophecy, and that the prayer of Hannah, Samuel's mother—
"The LORD kills and makes alive;
He brings down to the grave, and brings up"[a]—
celebrates the sons of Korah, who went down into the pit until their feet touched bottom, and then came up.[247]

Rabbah the son of Bar Hana recollected, "On a journey through the wilderness, my Arab guide asked me if I cared to see the place where Korah's men were swallowed up?
"I went.
"Smoke issued through a narrow fissure in the rock. The Arab soaked a scrap of fleece, attached it to his spear and passed it over the crack. Heat singed the wool.
"I told him: 'Listen.'
"Placing our ears as close to the earth as we dared, we heard this vocal chorus:
'Moses is truth. His Torah is truth. And we are liars.'"[248]

When God threatened to consume everyone along with Korah's party, Moses and Aaron together asked, "Shall one man sin, and You blast all Your children?"
According to Rabbi Nehemiah, those sons who did not honor their father Korah, or keep his counsel, answer Moses' and his brother's question:
"We saw the miracles He wrought for us.
When the earth's mouth gaped and swallowed
we rose on masts in space, and did not die, a sign
the righteous are not taken with the wicked,
as we were not."

---

a. 1 Samuel 2:6

STATUTE

MIRIAM'S STORY

ḤUKKAT/חקת—Numbers 19:1-22:1
The LORD spoke to Moses and to Aaron, saying:
This is the statute of the law which the LORD has commanded.

In the prologue to Exodus, a three-month-old boy of the house
of Levi is set adrift in a basket to preserve him from the death
Pharaoh decreed against all male Hebrew children. His sister
follows the baby downstream, watches Pharaoh's daughter
pluck her brother from the river reeds, and comes forward to
offer the child's own mother as wet-nurse.

Miriam is that sister, but neither her name, nor her parents'
identity, nor that of the boy-child's brother appear in the text
until God calls Moses back to Egypt from his forty-year exile in
Midian.

Moses speaks of Miriam by name four times in his Five Books.

In the first instance, Miriam the Prophetess, the sister of
Aaron picked up a hand-drum and danced and led the women of
Israel beside the Red Sea, answering Moses' triumphal song
with this chorus:

"Sing to the Name, the One who won

Has thrown horse and rider into the sea."[a]

The next episode occurs in the second year of Israel's
wilderness journey, when Miriam and Aaron grumbled against
Moses and asked, "Has the LORD only spoken through Moses?
Has he not also spoken through us?"

God heard, and came down in a pillar of cloud. Standing at
the door of the Tent, He called out Aaron and Miriam, and said,
"With Moses I speak mouth to mouth, not in dark speeches; and

a. Exodus 15:21

he beholds the likeness of the Unpronounceable. Did you not fear to speak against my servant Moses?"

The Presence departed and, Behold! Miriam was leprous, white as snow.

Aaron said to Moses, "We have done foolishly. But let her not be as one dead."

Moses cried, "Heal her now, O God."

And God replied, "Let her be shut outside the camp seven days." Miriam was shut out seven days; and the people did not journey until Miriam returned to them.[a]

Only in the third instance, in the fortieth year of their wanderings, in the genealogy that precedes the census taken in Moab on the banks of the Jordan, is Miriam fully identified as the sister of Aaron and Moses.[b]

Moses names Miriam a fourth and final time in Deuteronomy, when the Lawgiver warns Israel to "remember what the LORD thy God did unto Miriam by the way, after you came forth out of Egypt."[c]

The name מִרְיָם/Miriam joins the Hebrew root מַר/mar [bitter] with יָם/yam [great inland water or river]. The name recalls her presence at the river Nile; places her beside the Reed Sea at the well of Marah,[d] which is bitterness; and partakes of jealousy's bitter water.[e]

Their whole time in the Wilderness, Israel was accompanied by a spring that moved with them from place to place. Tradition records that God made this well on the second day of Creation. Just as manna satisfied their hunger, so the well slaked the people's thirst. Rav observed, "That would be

a. Numbers 12:1-16
b. Numbers 26:59
c. Deuteronomy 24:9
d. Exodus 15:23
e. Numbers 5:18

Miriam's well; a movable well cannot be unclean."

Miriam's well resembled a rock flask the size of a beehive; from its narrow mouth water spouted like drink from a wineskin.

The well rolled up mountains and down into valleys along with the congregation.

Wherever Israel camped, the well settled on a rise opposite the entrance to the Tent of Meeting. The princes of Israel would walk around the well with their staves and chant the song:

"Spring up, O well."

The waters then rose up like a pillar, and each prince dug a channel with his staff, directing the stream toward his tribe and family, who sang:

"The well the princes dug,
the nobles of their people delved
with sceptre and with staves."

The well's twelve streams flowed in all directions throughout the camp, and entered the surrounding wasteland. Its channels were so large that the Israelites used small boats to visit one another.[249]

When time came to move on, the people again sang to the well, and their praise set the well in motion.[250]

Avin the Levite said, "When Israel chanted the Song at the Red Sea,[a] Moses recited with them, the way a teacher tells a child, 'Repeat after me.' But after forty years in the Wilderness, Israel had learned their lesson, and chanted the Song of the Well on their own."[251]

Moses is not mentioned in their song.

Neither is the holy One, because God said, "If Moses is not mentioned, I will not be either."

---

a. Exodus 15:1-19

The people answered their Creator,
"It is your duty to perform miracles for us;
   it is ours to bless and praise the Name."[252]

When Miriam died, the well disappeared. The angry congregation marched on Moses and Aaron, who were busy about the details of their sister's funeral.

The brothers sought refuge in the Tent of Meeting. There, the glory of the One appeared and commanded his two servants, "Leave here, now. My children die from thirst, and you sit mourning that old woman?[253]

"Bring the people. I will give them water.

"You and your brother Aaron, take the rod. Speak to the rock before their eyes. It will spout water."

Moses struck the rock, twice, with his rod. The water came, but thanks to that that second stroke of doubt, Moses and his brother would not cross Jordan.

Then Israel sang: "Rise up, well!"

   Which well? They sung:
"Sing well, a song
   with Aaron's rod,
   by Moses' word,
the nobles they dug well."

Miriam's well accompanied the people all forty years' of their sojourn in the Wilderness. Their song appears in the text only in the last year of Israel's wanderings, when its waters quenched more than thirst.

Kings Sihon of the Amorites and Og of Bashan planned to ambush the tribes as they passed through the mountains between Moab and Canaan. Then, legend has it, God pushed the mountains of the Promised Land against the mountains of Moab, crushing those royal armies hidden in hillside caves. The well flooded the valley and flushed away the enemy's corpses while Israel passed by on a high road formed by the joined peaks, wonders equal to those seen at the Red Sea.

Late in the second century, after Bar Kochba's rebellion, Ḥiyya the Babylonian moved to Palestine. There, the rabbi reported, when you climb to the top of Mount Nebo (named for Babylon's god of scribes and wisdom[254]) you will see a small whirlpool in the Sea of Tiberias. This is Miriam's Well.[255]

Maimonides[256] regarded Miriam's death and burial as a form of modesty. The physician believed that a thoughtful person stricken with years and approaching death sees more of that which lies beyond words. Closer to the end, love for that unmediated truth becomes stronger, and the soul separates from the body in a moment of unspeakable pleasure. This is why the Sages[257] teach that Moses, Aaron and Miriam all died by a kiss. But where Moses and Aaron died by the mouth of the LORD, the same is not written of Miriam. That, our guide explains, is because Miriam was a woman, and the figurative expression "God's mouth" was unseemly when applied to her.

BALAK

A PROPHET LIKE NO OTHER AMONG THE NATIONS,
WHO HEARS GOD'S SPEECH

BALAK/בלק—Numbers 22:2-25:9
Balak son of Zippor saw all that Israel had done to the Amorites.

Balak, King of Moab, read in the stars that many in Israel
would fall by his hand, but did not understand how. So Balak
the seer sent for Balaam the prophet who, by speaking a word,
could uproot a whole nation.[258]

The Book of Yashar records that Balaam, Jethro priest of
Midian, and Job the Uzzite had each counseled Pharaoh when
he asked how to deal with Israel.

Jethro responded, "They are the chosen; do nothing. Let
them go forth to Canaan if you do not want them in Egypt."

Then Jethro fled.

Job answered Pharaoh, "All who inhabit the land are in
your power. Do whatever pleases you."

On the strength of this advice, the adversary, Satan, spoke
up when God asked the heavenly court, "Have you considered
my servant Job?"

Balaam told Pharaoh, "No matter what you do against the
Hebrews, they will be delivered. But if you command that all
their male children born from this day forward be drowned in
the river Nile, you can wipe out their name."

Balaam, son of בְּעוֹר/Beor, kin of בָּעַר/baar [to burn, consume].
Repoint the root and it becomes: בְּעֵור/beaar [of the blind or one-
eyed]; בְּעוּר/beur [roused awake, or bare, exposed]. "Beor" also
can mean, "in skin."

When Israel departed Egypt, Balaam tore at his flesh and
plucked out his hair and set off for the mountains of the East to

study sorcery and divination under Azazel and Uzza.

As told in the *Book of Splendor*, Uzza and Azazel were angels cast out of heaven. They fell to earth, espoused daughters of men, and seduced the world.[a] For this, God chained them to a mountain of darkness. Uzza resisted, so God bound him under the mountain, all light shut out. Because Azazel went quietly, God tethered him on the mountain slope where a dim ray leaked into his open eye.

In those days, Balaam was the only man left on earth who sought them out. A prophet like no other among the Nations, such as Moses was in Israel, Balaam styled himself "One who hears God's speech, and knows knowledge of the most High."

Rabbi Simeon agreed. "Oh yes, Balaam heard the words of a god—the one called 'another god'; and he had knowledge of the most High—the highest of the low. His vision of the Almighty was a vision of Uzza, the planet Venus, and of Azazel, the wilderness spirit to whom a scapegoat was sent on the Day of Atonement."

Abba the son of Kahana added, "The holy One examined Balaam and found him to be a sack of piss.

"When God asked who the men were with him, Balaam should have answered: 'Ruler of the Universe! 'Nothing is hidden from you, and you ask me?'

"But Balaam thought: 'He does not know! At times he does not know. I shall do as I please.'

"So this bladder replied: 'Balak son of Zippor, king of Moab, sent them. You may not honor me like Moses, but kings seek me out.'"[259]

Balak connived with Balaam, saying, "Let us drive Israel from the earth. Their strength is found in deeds and words, the

---

a. 1Enoch 8-10

same as ours.

"You say the words; I'll do the deeds."

Rabbi Simeon spat out, "Let them both rot in hell. The king's son bet on Balaam's sharp mouth and ready tongue. But God told the prophet, 'Curse Israel will you?

"'Eye open? let your eye fall out!'"[260]

After Balaam pronounced three blessings where he could not curse—

"How goodly are thy tents, O Jacob;"

"Who hath counted the dust of Jacob?" and

"None hath beheld iniquity in Jacob"—

he instructed Balak how to destroy Israel through the skin:

"In Egypt, these people dressed in linen garments. Where Jacob camps, erect some tents for selling linen. Partition them with curtains. Station old harlots out in front, and place your daughters behind the curtains.

"When an Israelite takes a stroll after his meal, have the old ones hawk linens at the going price. Young harlots in the back will offer the same wares at discount.

"After two or three sales, the have young say to each man, 'You are family. Come in. Sit down. Take what you desire.'

"From a cooler of Ammonite wine, she should fill his cup.

"Aroused, the Hebrew will say, 'I want you.'

"She then must draw the small carving from between her breasts, and murmur, 'First worship this.'

"He will protest, 'I am a Jew.'

"She will reply, 'So what? Uncover yourself. This is how I worship.'

"Naked, she must resist until the man rejects the Torah."[261]

Through Balaam's counsel, 24,000 of Israel perished.

When Balaam rode off with the princes of Moab, Gods anger burned, and the angel of the LORD placed himself in the way for an adversary. Balaam's ass saw the angel, the prophet did not.

Rashi understands this Satan to be an angel of mercy, who desired to restrain Balaam from committing a sin.

After God opened Balaam's eyes, the angel told the prophet, "I am as an adversary [לְשָׂטָן/l'satan] because your way is contrary; you arouse and provoke me."

Midrash Rabbah comments that the LORD opened Balaam's eyes to teach him that the eye, too, is in God's power.

Resh Laqish regarded Satan, the Evil Inclination, and the Angel of Death as three names for the same thing:

"He ascends and leads astray, ascends and accuses,
    obtains permission and takes the soul."[262]

The adversary, the dark urge, and death's angel may be one, but each has a different face and dwelling.

The Angel of Death goes by many names. It separates soul from body, and carries that plucked thing beyond report.

The יֵצֶר הָרַע/yetser ha-ra [the Evil Inclination] lives only in the human, body and soul, and has a human face.

Satan is an aspect of God, of baffled understanding. If the adversary were merely baleful, why did he oppose, rather than accuse or tempt Balaam?

Why else would Satan propose a wager when God asked (in another book tradition ascribes to Moses) if he had considered, cast his eye upon, "My servant Job, none like him in the earth, a plain and upright man?"[a]

What did Balak the son of Zippor see?

The Zohar says he watched, with his own eyes,
the tails of the stars skirt wisdom's windows
    and, through one window, heard light's open wing.
Balak, son of a bird ("Zippor"means "bird" in Hebrew), read
birds' flight like a book, by magic art.[263]

King David saw, and heard, and spoke against the liars, haters,
adversaries who give evil back for good, who fight and need no
cause, and prayed:
    "God, set an evil one above him;
    have Satan stand at his right hand."[a]

    I look to the sky, and wait
for a hand to reach down
through a window, a cloud,
    and I wait. Like drought land
rutted, cracked with contempt
for the easy, with scorn for the proud
tanning nude, we want rain.
    Tip your hand.
    We will wait.[b]

---

a. Psalm 109
b. Psalm 123

PHINEHAS

IS ELIJAH PHINEHAS? ALL ISRAEL USED TO SAY THAT HE IS

PINHAS/פינחס—Numbers 25:10-30:1
The LORD spoke to Moses, saying:
Phinehas, the son of Eleazar, the son of Aaron the priest,
has turned My wrath away from the children of Israel
by being so zealous among them for My sake
that I consumed them not in My jealousy.

Before he related the instructions for making burnt-offerings, Moses asked God to set a man over the congregation, "so they be not as sheep that have no shepherd."

The One told Moses to bring Joshua into the presence of the priest and the whole congregation, where "you will put your honor upon him"—some of your honor, but not all.

To tend religion, God leavened the rote of ritual with mortal zeal and gave the priesthood to the javelin-wielding Levite Phinehas and his descendants.

Of transmitted wisdom, the elders of the generation which crossed Jordan used to say,

"Moses' face shone like the sun,

but Joshua's face is merely the moon.

Faded glory. What a comedown."

About Pinhas' everlasting priesthood, they held their peace.

The Sages wondered why the daily burnt sacrifices and a second set of Temple offerings for Sabbath and other occasions commanded in Numbers are identical to those ordained in Exodus.[a]

Rabbi Aha held that the ordinance was repeated because, when the Temple stood and received their offerings, Israel

---

a. Exodus 29:38-42

studied the pertinent rituals.

Lacking both Temple and altar for the sacrifice, Israel wondered, "Why review the practice?"

The Creator answered, "When you study my instruction, you observe the offerings."

Moses was taken aback when commanded: "Food of sweet savor prepare and offer up to Me in due season."

The man asked, "LORD, were I to bring all the beasts of the earth, would they suffice for a single offering? or if I brought every tree in this world, would that be enough to build one altar fire?"

God reassured him, "Moses, it is not as you think. Just offer he-lambs of the first year without blemish, two day by day; not even two at a time; but one in the morning, and the other lamb offer up at dusk."[264]

According to Rabban Gamaliel, the two lambs for the Sabbath correspond to the two worlds, this world and the world to come. The Zohar counsels, "Worship and pray twice, with Gladness and singing, two prayers, two daily offerings:

"Gladness in the morning, singing in the evening."

The Faithful Shepherd teaches that, when עֹלַת תָּמִיד/olat tamid—a continual burnt offering for a sweet savor unto the LORD—is made evening and morning, the same as we say

"Hear, O Israel," twice every day

its scent rises all the way to the Most High.

And what is this ascent?

The savor, a ladder by which all beings ascend and descend.[265]

Tradition asserts that Pinḥas and Elijah are the same person.

Rabbi Eliezer taught that God called Phineḥas by Elijah's

name because the prophet brought about Israel's repentance in Gilead, and slew Baal's prophets with a sword. For this, Elijah received both the life of this world and of the world to come:[a] a covenant of life and peace. To Pinḥas and his sons God gave a good reward, the everlasting priesthood: His covenant of peace.

In the chapter "Inappropriate Calmness,"[266] Avraham ben Rambam asserts that calmness is only necessary when personal concerns and worldly desires are at stake, not when there is a religious issue. He cites Pinḥas as one zealous and passionate for a religious purpose, and then Elijah the Prophet, who slaughtered 450 idolatrous prophets within a short period of time, saying, 'I am exceedingly jealous for God.'[b]

"And do not challenge me for listing Elijah after Pinḥas," Maimonides' son argues, "basing your objection on the teaching that these two men were one and the same. If this is true, it reinforces the evidence of his religious jealousy, but if he is in fact a different man," as Avraham's own father maintained in the Mishneh Torah, "then both were jealous for God."

Rabbi Eleazar and Rabbi Yose were walking in the Wilderness. Yose said, "When God says of Phineḥas,

'Behold, I give him my covenant of peace,'
it means, peace from the Angel of Death, so that he should never have power over Phineḥas and so that he should never suffer death's chastisements. As for the tradition that Pinḥas did not die, the truth is he did not die like other men. He outlived all his generation, and departed from the world with celestial yearning and beauteous attachment."[267]

---

a. 1Kings 17:1-19:2; 2Kings 1:1-2:14
b. 1Kings 19:1

In the *Book of Lineage*, Abraham Zacuto reasoned as follows: "Elijah is still alive. Thus, he is not identical with Phineḥas."

But Levi bar Gershom countered, "Elijah is Phineḥas, and all Israel used to say that he is Phineḥas, so the problem is not solved.

"May he come soon and tell the answer."

TRIBES

MOSES ABSOLVES GOD OF HIS OATH TO DESTROY ISRAEL,
BUT QUESTIONS REMAIN

MATTOT/מטות—Numbers 30:2-32:42
Moses spoke to the heads of the tribes of the children
of Israel, saying:
This is the thing the LORD has commanded.[a]

The prophet Joel declares that, on the Day of Judgment, God will make wars to cease, and will judge all the nations round about.[b]

In a discourse of Rav Kahana, Israel asks, "How will this judgment be carried out?"

The One replies, "All will be left to you. You will have authority to impose any form of death you wish.

"You will avenge the blood.[c] Anyone who waged war against you has warred against me."

God said the same to Moses: "Avenge the children of Israel of the Midianites; afterward shalt thou be gathered unto thy people."

To make explicit that they acted on God's behalf, Moses told Israel, "Execute the LORD's vengeance on Midian."

To that end, Moses dispatched a thousand men of war from every tribe, along with Phineḥas, the high priest Eleazar's zealot son, who bore the Ark, the holy vessels, and the trumpets. They slew every male, the five kings of Midian, and Balaam the son of Beor. The army captured all the women of Midian and all their little ones, all their cattle, all their flocks, and all their goods. They burned all the Midianite cities and

---

a. Numbers 30:1 KJV
b. Joel 4:12/ KJV 3:12
c. Numbers 35:15

encampments with fire.

When the twelve tribes' captains brought their spoils to Moses in the plains of Moab near Jericho, he erupted, "You have saved the very women who enticed twenty-four thousand men of Israel to their destruction?

"Now go. Kill every male among the little ones, and every woman old enough to know a man.

"All the female children too young to have known a man, keep for yourselves.

"Then pitch your tents outside the encampment seven days. Anyone who has killed a person, or touched the dead, must purify himself, and his captives, and clothing, and implements of war."

On this day before his death, Moses grew so angry that he forgot the purification ritual for unclean metal utensils, and it fell to the high priest to instruct the army. "This is the statute of the Law which God commanded Moses," Eleazar told the troops, meaning, "God commanded them through Moses, He did not command through me."[268]

Before he ordered the tribes to take vengeance upon Midian, Moses taught their chiefs the rules for keeping and annulling oaths and vows.

The same rules applied when, as Berekiah tells it, the people made and worshipped the molten calf. Atop Sinai, the Lawgiver argued that God should not destroy Israel, but forgive them.

God said, "Moses, I have already taken an oath,[a] and I cannot retract an oath which has gone from my mouth."

Moses countered, "Maker of All, you taught me that, when

---

a. Exodus 22:19

a man vows a vow or swears an oath he shall not break his word, but another may absolve him." Moses wrapped himself in his sage's cloak and sat while God stood before him as does the petitioner asking the rabbinic court for annulment of a vow.

Huna son of Aḥa remarked, "It was hard for Moses to annul God's vow."

Rabbi Yoḥanan agreed, "Very hard. Moses had to ask, 'Do you regret?'

"God answered, 'I now regret the evil which I said I would do unto my people.'[a]

"Then Moses ruled, 'Be it absolved for thee. Be it absolved for thee. There is no longer oath nor vow.'"

Simeon ben Laqish added, "Because Moses absolved God's vow, in Psalm 90 he is called a man or spouse of God."[269]

Another proposed that Moses was called God's spouse because he was like a husband who, if he wants to, cancels his wife's vow, and if he wants to keep it, lets it stand.

The psalm begins: A prayer of Moses, a man of God.
The midrash asks: If man, how God? If God, how man?

Rabbi Abin explained, "Above his waist Moses was called God. From his waist down he was a man."

Eliezer the Great mapped the four quarters of the created world.

From the one that faces east, light goes forth.

From the south-facing quarter, dews of blessing fall.

From the west, the treasuries of snow and hail, come cold, heat and rain.

The quarter facing north, God created but did not complete.

He said, "Anyone who declares 'I am a god,' let him finish this."

---

a. Exodus 32:14

In the north, the agents of destruction dwell. From the north, as Jeremiah prophesied, evil breaks forth.[270]

In the ninth year of Zedekiah's reign, in the tenth month, in the tenth day of the month, Nebuchadnezzar king of Babylon came with all his host against Jerusalem. Famine prevailed, there was no bread for the people, and all the men of war fled by night.[a]

The king put the Temple's servants to the sword. God took no pity upon any, young or old, man or maiden, infant or one stooped for age, but gave all into the Chaldees' hand. They captured Zedekiah and his sons in the plain near Jericho, and brought them to the king, who slew the sons in their father's presence, then put out the Zedekiah's eyes.

Nebuchadnezzar burnt the house of God, broke down the wall, razed the palaces with fire, and destroyed everything not taken as spoil. His army carried off to Babylon the instruments and vessels in God's house, all Jerusalem's treasures along with a remnant who escaped the sword to serve him and his sons, "To fulfil the word of the LORD by the mouth of Jeremiah."[b]

King David's court musician Asaph sang:
"The nations are come into your inheritance;
    they have defiled your holy temple."[c]
God replied, "I commanded them to do so, saying
'I will call all the families of the kingdoms of the north,
and they will come, and they shall set every one his throne
at the entrance of the gates of Jerusalem.'[d]
"And," God continued, "what did the nations do?

---

a. 2Kings 25:1-10
b. 2Chronicles 36:17-21
c. Psalm 79:1
d. Jeremiah 1:15

They made Jerusalem into heaps,[a] but I shall set it up anew."
 Yet Asaph wondered, "Master of the Universe,
You will renew the heaps, but your children who were slain,
 what of them?"[271]

---

a. Jeremiah 9:11

JOURNEYS

NO RECORD OF TIME OR DISTANCE BETWEEN ISRAEL'S CAMPSITES DURING
THIRTY-EIGHT YEARS OF WANDERING

MASE'EI/מסעי—Numbers 33:1-36:13
These are the journeys of the children of Israel,
by which they marched out of the land of Egypt;
And Moses wrote their goings forth, stage by stage,
as directed by the LORD.

The rock we stand on is the rock
We sing to: deep as well shafts
High as glacier tops: the land
We live on and the ocean smaller
Only than the sky that rests inside
Its cup:
        A heart is harder
Than the wilderness our fathers
Wandered, proof that they were
Human, bitter like the aftertaste
Of water in a mouth turned forty
That has never kissed except
In lust, or rage, or envy, after
Wanting, wanting, and no rest.[a]

When Israel left Rameses—"child of the sun," the Egyptians
wept and buried their dead while the Israelites sang:
    "The right hand of the LORD is exalted."[b]
They camped at Succoth—"booths," which some say is a place
name like Etham where Israel stopped next, though Akiba
claims Succoth means "clouds of glory."[c] [272]

a. Psalm 95
b. Psalm 118:16
c. Isaiah 4:5-6

From Etham the multitude turned back from the Wilderness into "the place where sedge grows" or "mouth of the gorges," where they left Pharaoh's armies and passed through the sea.

In the Wilderness they stopped in Marah—of the "bitter" waters; at the oasis Elim—"palms"; then by the Reed Sea.

They pitched their tents in the wilderness of Sin—of "thorn" or "clay"—at places called "knocking," "I will knead bread," and "rests" (a place without water).

Then Israel camped at Sinai—"thorny," and received the Law.

Next they journeyed to "graves of longing," "settlement," and Rithmah—"heath," where the spies brought back an evil report of the Promised Land.

From Rithmah, until the fortieth year after the Exodus when Israel came to Mount Hor, the stages for thirty-eight years of wanderings are unmarked by date or length of stay. But a whisper of experience attends the roll, even in translation: 'pomegranate of the breach"; "pavement"; "ruin"; "assembly"; "beauty"; "fear"; "assembly place"; "station"; "delay"; "sweetness"; "fatness"; "bonds"; "sons of twisting"; "cave of the gap"; "pleasantness"; "passage"; "a man's backbone"—last stop before the place named "holy" in the wilderness of "flat."

Aaron died at Horeb, on the border of Edom, where Moses' telling re-enters time and the map. The tribes camped at "shady"; at "darkness" or "perplexity"; at "waterskins"; at "ruins" of "regions beyond"; at "wasting"; at "hiding the two cakes" close to Moab.

In the mountains of Abarim, Israel pitched tents by Nebo—"prophet"; near Jericho—"fragrant," they camped beside Jordan, from the "house of desolation" to the "meadow of acacias" in the plains "of his father," and the LORD spoke.

Moses' tally of Israel's forty-two stopping places between Egypt and Canaan does not conjure up a spectacle like Homer's catalogue of ships. It wants the pride and blood of the epic poet's genealogies; it cannot offer the shared inheritance and hopes that inform the enumeration of the tribes exiting Egypt and entering Canaan.

The stage names are sounds, place-holders for what must be so but can't be known, a mirage of meaning.

A Medieval Jewish spell to drive out the demon of forgetfulness at the end of Sabbath involves reciting the demon's name over and over, each time decreasing the name by a letter, until (according to Rashi) the demon shrinks and finally vanishes.[273] In the Wilderness, as the stages are chanted, the generation of the Exodus disappears, one-by-one or in companies. Aaron and the clouds of glory vanish at mount Hor, and Moses dies in Moab, the prophet whom the LORD knew face to face.

In the chapter "Poetic Wisdom," Giambattista Vico explains that gentile gods spoke in lightning hiss and thunderclap. Their divine speech was made intelligible by poet-sages through their science, called the Muses. Homer defined those Nine daughters of Memory as the knowledge of good and evil—that fruit which God forbade to Adam. Fear of the divine thunderbolt created those "other" gods. The fear did not originate in the other, though; that fear was awakened by men in themselves. Gentile sages fashion oracles and stories of their gods from "the credible impossibility":[274] what seems real, but cannot be.

In rabbinic legend, God told Moses, "All those years in the Wilderness, I cast down your enemies just by being with you.

Snakes and scorpions live there, but I did not let them harm
you. Now, write down the stages of Israel's journey in the
Wilderness, so they know what miracles I wrought for them."[275]

That is, Moses was commanded to set down the incredible
possibility: what cannot be, but is.

Unlike creation, which is present, or stories of the Fall, the
Flood, the confusion of tongues, the lives of the Patriarchs, and
the going-out from Egypt, thirty-eight years in the wasteland
made no news or law or image or echo. Absent the testimony of
other witnesses, Maimonides remarked that any attempt by
Moses to imaginatively recreate this period might be mistaken
for a fairy tale.[276]

The Wilderness is like science's black box. The going in
and coming out are known. But in between? The people had to
eat and drink those forty years. The surrounding narrative
implies that children were born, even as the older generation
died. And Rabbis have deduced from the mention of twelve
water springs and seventy date palms in Elim that Israel only
camped near water.

What served as food each day for all those thousands
numbered by Moses and Eleazar beside Jordan?

Reason, speaking from its own extremity, can only answer:
Miracle. Manna fed them in the waste.

Deuteronomy

THESE, THE WORDS

GOD'S LONG SILENCE IN THE WILDERNESS, AND THE SONG MOSES SANG
WHEN GIVEN LEAVE

DEVARIM/דברים—Deuteronomy 1:1-3:22
These are the words which Moses spoke to all Israel
this side Jordan, in the Wilderness,...
In the fortieth year.

There is a gap in the biblical chronology between the last verse of Deuteronomy 1 and the first verse of the following chapter.

From the Ninth of Av, in the second year of Israel's departure from Egypt, until the fortieth year when God told Moses "You have circled this mountain long enough," Moses wrote nothing.

On that Ninth of Av, the spies returned from Canaan with a fearful report. Israel believed the spies, and doubted the Promised Land was good. The angry One then decreed that, except for Joshua and Caleb, not one man of that generation would live to see the land flowing with milk and honey.

Only the children would inherit.

For Israel, the sentence meant aimless wandering.

For Moses, God's anger is more personal. The Lawgiver would not enter the land. Also, during those lost years, God kept silent.

What did Moses do in the silence?

One legend tells that on the eve of the Ninth of Av, every year for thirty-eight years, Moses sent a herald throughout the camp, who proclaimed: "Go out. Dig your grave. Go out. Dig your grave!"

The people went out. Each dug a grave, lay down in it, and spent the night.

Next morning the herald cried: "Let the living leave the dead!"

The living stood up.

Each morning, on the Ninth of Av, fifteen thousand rose no more. And so it went, year after year.

In the last year of their wanderings, the children of Israel dug graves, and spent the night.

Next morning, all arose. None had died.[277]

That same day, when all the generation were consumed and dead, God broke silence and spoke again to Moses.

First, the holy One issued marching orders for Israel's conquest of the lands and peoples east of Jordan.

Then, He removed Moses from the leadership of Israel, and bestowed it upon Joshua.

And here the Torah portion stops.

The Sabbath preceding the Ninth of Av, Tisha B'Av, is called the Sabbath of Vision, after Isaiah's vision of the destruction of the Temple and the sack of Jerusalem.

Isaiah testifies by sound, not sight:

"Hear, O heavens, and give ear, O earth,
for the LORD hath spoken."[a]

His call echoes the opening of the Song of Moses:

"Give ear, o ye heavens, and I will speak;
and hear, o earth, the words of my mouth."[b]

Where Moses' testimony is direct, the words of a man who, even when his prayer is denied, is heard, Isaiah's words are of the One removed, transmitted from afar.

In an opportune moment, William Blake asked Isaiah how he could be certain that the voice he heard was God's.

a. Isaiah 1:2
b. Deuteronomy 32:1

The prophet answered the poet:
"I saw no God, nor heard any, in a finite organical perception;
    but my senses discoverd the infinite in every thing,
    and as I was then perswaded, & remain confirmd,
    that the voice of honest indignation is the voice of God,
I cared not for consequences but wrote."[278]

The First Temple was destroyed because of three evils in it: idolatry, immorality, and bloodshed.

When it fell, prophecy ceased. In the prophetic silence, some read history for signs.

The Second Temple also fell on the Ninth of Av, even though people studied Torah, observed the commandments, and practiced charity.

Why? A later generation[279] holds that while the Second Temple stood, hatred without rightful cause prevailed. Hatred without rightful cause is as grave as the sins of idolatry, immorality, and bloodshed combined.

By Hadrian's imperial decree, Jerusalem was plowed under, on Tisha B'Av, 130 C.E.

There is no Temple now.

There is Jerusalem.

There is still hatred without rightful cause.

Who doesn't deem his hatred rightful?

And there is silence.

Besides the countless blessings the One showered on Israel recorded by Moses, the prophet and teacher and lawgiver bestowed four of his own.

Two of those blessings are found in Deuteronomy: the first, "The LORD, God of your fathers, make you a thousand so many more as ye are, and bless you;" and the fourth, "and this the blessing wherewith Moses the man of God blessed the children of Israel before his death."[a]

The second blessing appears in Leviticus,[b] when Moses and Aaron come out from the Tent of Meeting and bless the people.

After the people finished constructing the Sanctuary, in Exodus, Moses blessed Israel a third time,[c] saying, "May the Presence rest upon the work of your hands" and, the man continued, in the words of the psalm[d] he composed:

Lord, where we have always lived
Before the earth and sun were born,
You made us children of destruction
And ask us to return again, return
Although an eye blinks and a thousand
Years pass, though the night watch hours
Creep crawl to eternity. Days crest
Past on the sweeping flood, sleep
To the sleepless, no sooner grown then mown
Grass, clippings blown across the walk.
Your anger wind time swallows up
Our secrets, whistles through our faults,
Our faces masks worn in a tale
Seventy or eighty years (that's
For the lucky) told in work and tears.
How strong's the wind? More than we fear.
So teach us how to weigh a day,

a. Deuteronomy 33:1
b. Leviticus 9:23
c. Exodus 39:43
d. Psalm 90

To wear the burden of a heart.
Because we do not know how long
Before we must return, Lord,
Damp the dust with small rain, shade
The strong sun behind towered clouds
Sometimes, so that our children know
A dappled place much like our fathers had,
But happy, not the evil we have learned
To handle, greedy factories of hate,
And let some part of what we've made last
Touch upon you, that part
A heart or hand has made.

I PLEADED

THE SOUND OF GOD'S VOICE ON SINAI, AND GOD'S LAST WORD TO MOSES ON A BITTER MATTER

VA-'ETḤANNAN/ואתחנן—Deuteronomy 3:23-7:11
I pleaded with the LORD at that time.

Moses implored God to let him enter the promised Land.

God answered, "Enough. Not another word to me about this matter. Ever."

Ḥanina bar Papa said, "In Deuteronomy, the One spoke to Israel פָּנִים בְּפָנִים/panim b·panim [face to face]. Panim, a plural, has no singular form. So, face to face implies at least four faces:

an awe-inspiring face—Scripture;
an even-tempered face—Mishnah;
a friendly face—Talmud;
a joyous face—Aggadah."

On Sinai the people heard a great voice. After that first voice, they felt great fear, and said to Moses,

"Behold, the LORD hath shown us his glory.

Now wherefore should we die?

"Go thou near and hear."

The *Book of Beliefs and Opinions* describes the angel sent by the Creator to separate soul from body. The messenger appears before the dying person as a figure of yellowish fire filled with eyes of bluish fire; his hand holds a drawn sword aimed at the one still alive. When he sees the angel, the person shudders, and his spirit departs.

How does the soul appear?

In the *Zohar Ḥadash*, the soul derives from understanding, which dwells above, in thought, and has no end. Understanding knows no image, no form, or likeness, because it is the world to come. The soul becomes visible, a midrash[280] says, "when you observe those words the LORD spoke to the congregation"—"those words" being the Commandments.

Some precepts are a burden, some are light.

Simeon the son of Yoḥai taught: "The lightest duty bids you let the mother go, should you happen on a bird's nest.[a]

"The most burdensome commands you to honor your father and your mother."

According to Ḥiyya bar Abba, "Whenever someone recites the *Shema*—

'Hear O Israel, the LORD our God, the LORD is one'—

it is as if he had kept all Ten Commandments, which God spoke at the hour prescribed for the *Shema*."

The morning of the Gathering at Mount Sinai was a day of clouds, of mist and a light rain. God spoke to Moses alone.

Moses then went to the foot of the mountain and communicated to the people what he heard.

About their hearing the great voice, Scripture says: "You heard the voice of the words, but you saw no figure, only a voice." It does not say, "You heard the words."

Thus, Maimonides reasons, all Israel heard only the sound of the voice.

But Moses heard articulate words, and reported them.[281]

A tradition among the Sages holds that the Israelites heard the first two commandments directly from the mouth of the Almighty, all in one sound, a sound such as mortal mouth cannot make nor mortal ears can hear, the sound of "a mighty

---

a. Deuteronomy 22:7

voice which cannot be exceeded."[282]

Of this voice Psalm 62 says: "One thing God has spoken; two things have I heard."

Naḥmanides maintains that the people heard all Ten Commandments directly when "The LORD spoke those words to your whole congregation, and He inscribed them on two tablets of stone." This means Moses inscribed on the tablets what God said to Israel's whole congregation, since "heard" includes both the hearing of the ear, and the understanding of the heart.[283]

Rabbi Yehudah observed, "A man speaking is visible, but his voice is invisible. In Exodus, however, that generation heard the voice of the One on Mount Sinai and saw the voice going forth from the mouth of Power in lightning and thunder.

"Otherwise, they saw nothing."[284]

Akiba said, "Israel saw and heard that which was visible.

"They saw the fiery word come out the mouth of the Almighty as it was struck upon the tablets, as David sings:

'The LORD's voice hewed out flames of fire.'"[a]

Rabbi Ishmael wondered, "How many thunderings were there, how many lightnings?

"No number. Simply this: they were heard by each soul according to his capacity."

Was there any pause between lightning and thunder?

In one account, when the Israelites stood before Sinai to receive the Torah, they interpreted the divine word the instant they heard it.[285]

The *Zohar Ḥadash* explains that Moses wrote "All the people saw" rather than "All the people heard" because, at first,

---

a. Psalm 29:7

sounds were not heard at all. Rather, as the ten utterances came forth, everyone would greet each utterance by kissing it softly. Only then would the commandment speak out and proclaim itself.[286]

Ibn Ezra glosses "Saw the sounds" as the application of a single verb to all the senses.

Exodus commands: "Remember the Sabbath day, to keep it holy."

In Deuteronomy, "Remember" becomes "Observe."

The Zohar makes this distinction: Observance concerns the heart. Therefore, "Observe" refers to the heart, and not to any other place. Memory concerns only the brain, which rides upon and dominates the heart. Therefore, "remember" refers to the brain.[287]

The *Pesikta Rabbati* interprets "Remember" as addressed to the nations of the world (who are aware of, but don't observe, the Sabbath). "Keep" is addressed to Israel.

Concerning the voices of the Giving of the Torah, an ḥasidic tradition teaches: "The Name with a mighty voice."

Onkelos translates the Hebrew of "with a mighty voice" into Aramaic as "He did not stop." That is, the voices remain today as they were then.

But now, as then, one must prepare to hear them.[288]

Alone. No help. But why so far?
To damp my roaring? Day or night,
Still out of earshot, tired of hearing
My complaint? But you're not crushed.
My father's father's father trusted
From his lamplit study, and was not

Unready. So I am less observant,
Less in learning, than the old ones. Smirkers
Bother now to point the finger. Teeth bared,
Lip curled, they shake their heads and mutter:
That one trusted in disorder, in the great
Provider: let his providence deliver him.

But you delivered me into the world,
Made hope the milk I drank, cradled me
Between your elbow crook and wrist,
Held up my head until I found my strength.
Support me now, when troubles
Ring me, paw like highland bulls, snort
Steam and heave fat divots with their hooves.
You must be near, must pick me up
And give me strength to save my life from bitterness.

If I have blown the horn of what I have imagined
To be true, it came from you. And shuddered.
Fear is praise to one who shows his face,
Who hears his name called in an empty place,
A name not known. Who but the meek
Could eat and not want more? The fat sit down
At groaning tables and remember to recall their souls.
While every time a world ends, seeds
Drop in the dust, then sprout, and someone
Else is born to care for what's beyond
Bad dreams. I live. The unborn queue.[a]

---

a. Psalm 22

BECAUSE

TWO KINDS OF REASONS

'EKEV/עקב—Deuteronomy 7:12-11:25
And it shall come to pass, because you hearken
to these ordinances, and keep, and do them...

There are two Torahs: the first tables of the Law, the work of God with the writing of God;[a] and the second Torah, also written by God, but on stone hewn by Moses and placed in an ark Moses made. There are two traditions, written and oral. There are two languages, public and private. Some words are written on gates, and some in the heart.

There are two kinds of "because."

The first kind, כִּי/ki, is a particle which places two things in relation, as in the Legend of the Fall when God says to the serpent, "Because thou has done this;" or to Adam, the first person, "Because thou hast hearkened unto the voice of thy wife."

The other "because"—עֵקֶב/ekev—entails a promise with consequences.

"Ekev" appears five times in the five Books of Moses:
in Genesis, after the binding of Isaac, when God blesses Abraham and his seed and all the earth, saying,
    "Because thou hast obeyed my voice,"
and again, when God repeats the blessing for Isaac,
    "Because Abraham obeyed my voice...;"[b]
in Numbers, after the spies' return from Canaan, when the One decrees that only Caleb shall enter the promised land
    "Because he was filled with a different spirit

---

a. Exodus 32:16
b. Genesis 22:18; 26:5

and has followed me...;"[a]
and in Deuteronomy, twice, where Moses interprets the legal
boundary of Israel's promised blessing:

"Because ye hearken to these ordinances, and keep, and do
them,...the LORD thy God shall keep with thee the covenant
and the mercy which he swore unto thy fathers, and he will love
thee, and bless thee, and multiply thee; But, ...if thou forget the
LORD thy God, and walk after other gods, and serve, and
worship them, I testify against you this day that ye shall surely
perish...

"Because ye would not hearken unto the voice
of the LORD your God."

Moses asks, "What does the LORD thy God require of thee?"

Rational law, which demands justice, good actions, and
recognizes God's bounty, rules every community. Judah Halevi
explained that the Torah God gave Israel is corollary to rational
law. Without their knowing how, the Presence descended on
Israel and God's fire consumed their offerings. Israel heard God
speak, heard the story of their becoming a people—all matters
which reason would refuse, were they not affirmed by
observance.

"Is it enough," Halevi asked, "for Jews to practice 'the
doing of justice and the love of mercy'? Can they neglect
circumcision, Sabbath, and other laws, and still feel happy?"[289]

According to Ḥanina bar Papa, the angel of conception is
named Night. "Night takes each human seed, places it before
the holy One and says, 'Master of the universe, what will this
drop become? A strong person or weak? a sage? a fool? rich?
poor?'

"The angel does not ask: 'Righteous or wicked.'

a. Numbers 14:22-24

"Why? Because everything is in the hands of Heaven, except the fear of Heaven."[290]

Moses' speech to the children of Israel modulates between the intimate and the public, a tonal shift marked in Hebrew by his use of the second person singular and plural. The distinction survives in the King James Version English, which uses the singular "thou-thee-thy" and the plural form "ye-you-your." "He said to me" sounds different depths than "He said to us."

When God threatened to destroy Israel for worshipping the Golden Calf, Moses spoke for the defense. He argued that while he, Moses, had received the commandments and so had not transgressed, yet the people have been given no commands, and therefore did not know.

God inquired, "Moses, have they not been commanded?"

Moses answered, "No. At Sinai you declared, 'I am the LORD thy God,'[a] not 'I am the LORD your God.'

"Next, you said 'Thou'—not 'ye'—'shalt have no other gods.'

"You addressed me as 'thou,' in the singular, not them as 'ye,' in the plural."[291]

Moses then took the second Tables of the Law, descended Sinai, and said to Israel, "These are the words which the LORD commanded, that ye should do them."[b]

Sifre Deuteronomy takes "You shall be mindful of this entire instruction" to mean, "embrace all of it:" learn interpretation, as well as Law and legends.

Moses taught, "Man does not live by bread alone"—by commentaries only—"but by everything that proceeds out of

a. Exodus 20:2
b. Exodus 35:1

the mouth of the LORD man lives"—by laws and legends.[292]
    To which Rabbi Ḥiyya[293] added, "God told Israel:
'Keep all this commandment, and you will be kept.'"
    So, Abba offered, "That is why we sing,
'Fear of the LORD is the beginning of wisdom.'"[a]
    And Rabbi Judah answered, "Serve the LORD
with gladness—with gladness comes a willing heart."[294]

> It helps to make a lot of noise
> When on the earth. We did not,
> Were modest, too, until God made us
> Enter squally bawling thank-yous
> In our lifetime, children's children.[b]

---

a. Psalm 111:10
b. Psalm 100

SEE

RE'EH/ראה—Deuteronomy 11:26-16:17
See, I set before you this day a blessing and a curse.

Before dismissing his children from the Wilderness and sending them into the world of strangers, Moses warned them, "All the matter which I command you, that you shall observe to do; do not add to it nor withdraw from it."

But Solomon took it upon himself to hallow the middle court and slaughter sacrifices other than on the altar; he also added to the sanctuary built in the desert, and omitted from it. David and Samuel appointed the order of the Temple choir. All these changes were undertaken in Jerusalem.

The king of the Khazars wondered how these actions could be reconciled with the order not to add to or diminish the law of Moses.

Judah Halevi's rabbi answered that this prohibition was addressed only to the masses, so that they would not conjecture or theorise or contrive laws of their own conception. They were to heed the prophets, and to respect priests and judges, whose decisions are binding.[295]

In his double Diaspora, Maimonides reasoned that God must know some matters of his Law would be added to or subtracted from in response to the needs of diverse places, events, and the force of circumstance. But he forbade addition or subtraction to forestall both corruption of the Law and belief that the Torah did not come from God. Men of knowledge are permitted to strengthen the Law through new interpretations, to build a hedge around the Torah. By the same token, in difficult situations they may suspend actions prescribed by Law or permit things forbidden by it, but such circumstantial measures may not be perpetuated.[296]

According to rabbinic tradition,[297] when God said: "See, I set before you this day a blessing and a curse," it meant that the Unpronounceable gave Israel blessings and curses not to hurt them, but rather to show them the way to the good.

Rabbi Haggai added, "Even more, not only does He set paths before us, but also God does not judge us by the strict letter of the law. We are told: 'Choose life.'"[a]

The sages of Yemen taught that on this, his last day, Moses advised Israel to repent, "so that your peace be like a river."[b]

Like a river?

Rabbi Ḥanina explained that towns served by a well invite disputes. "One person says, 'I will draw first;' another says, 'No, me.' But in a city beside a river, each person fills his cask, then goes his own way. What peace is better?"

When Moses spoke of what shall come to pass when the LORD your God brings you into the land, he told Israel, four times, "You shall pass over," to emphasize that "You, not I," will cross the Jordan. The Lawgiver hoped the people would plead on his behalf as he had prayed for them.

They did not.

Disappointed, Moses urged, "For your own sakes, observe to do all the commandments I set before you this day." In the land across the river (where he would not go), destroy all those places where the nations served their gods and idols. Then you, Israel, will come to "the place the LORD your God shall choose as a dwelling for his Name," the same high place Abraham saw

a. Deuteronomy 30:19
b. Isaiah 48:18

far off, where he bound Isaac to the altar, looked up and saw a ram to sacrifice.

Abraham called the place יְרָאֶה ׀ יְהוָה/Adonai Yireh [the LORD sees].[a] In that same place Noah's son Shem, the King Melchizedek,[b] blessed Abram, and called his city שָׁלֵם/Salem [Peace]. About that place, God reasoned,

"If I call my dwelling Yireh, Shem will resent it.

"If I name my city Salem, Abraham will feel slighted. So I will call my place Jerusalem—He will see peace."[298]

Berekiah added that, "while the place was still called Salem, God made himself a tabernacle there and prayed,

'O that I may see the Temple building.'[c]

So, after Abraham sacrificed the ram, he saw the Temple built, destroyed, and built again."

Now, everyone has seen the second destruction.

The plan for the Third Temple is laid out in Ezekiel's vision of a city[d] named שָׁמָּה ׀ יְהוָה/adonai shammah [the LORD is there]. According to the School of Elijah, in that place, in those days to come, the righteous will be given a new heart with an impulse to good, not to evil. God will remove the stony heart, and replace it with a heart of flesh.

Ezekiel's repetition of new heart and heart of flesh[e] follows the pattern established in the Five Books of Moses, where time and again matters are repeated as God reaches out toward man, and man reaches out toward God.[299]

The moment Israel heard the "I" of "I am the LORD your God"—the first word of the Ten Commandments—their

a. Genesis 22:14
b. Genesis 14:18
c. Psalm 76:3
d. Ezekiel 40-48
e. Ezekiel 18:31; 11:19; 36:26

souls left them.

That first word returned at once to the Creator and said, "Master of all, you live and last.

"The Torah lives and endures. Why send me to the dead? Can they hear?"

So, for His people's sake the One returned and sweetened the "I." He tuned his voice to the strength[a] of each listener— young, old, little ones, infants, grown men and women—so each heard only so much as he could bear.

"Not so," Rabbi Simeon objected.

"First the Torah told the holy One, 'The world rejoices for my sake, yet your children are dying.'

"With this, their souls returned. The Law restores souls."[b]

In another version, after Israel's souls decamped, the angels began to hug and kiss and reassure them, cooing, "What's this? Don't fear, you children of the LORD your God;" while the Maker repeated his word softly, saying, "I am your God as you are my beloved."

He coaxed until their souls returned.[300]

When God instructed Moses, "Go, tell Israel:

'You shall walk after the LORD your God,'"
the people replied, "Moses, who can walk after the LORD?

"Is not his way the whirlwind and the storm?[c]

"Is his way not in the sea, his path in the great waters? and his footsteps are not known."[d]

Rabbi Hama, son of Rabbi Ḥanina, wondered how to obey the commandment to walk behind the LORD, when the

---

a. Psalm 29:4
b. Psalm 19:8
c. Nahum 1:3
d. Psalm 77:20

Presence is a devouring fire?[a]

His father offered Moses' answer: "All God's paths are mercy and truth, acts of kindness and the Law."[301]

Maimonides took "walk behind" to mean following obediently His commandments and conducting life in accordance with His teaching. The philosopher also advocated imitating God's acts,[302] a prescription that would vary with one's abilities, and how much truth and goodness a person can bear.

---

a. Deuteronomy 4:24

JUDGES
BECAUSE THE WICKED PROSPER IN THIS WORLD, AND BECAUSE THE RIGHTEOUS SUFFER

SHOFETIM/שפטים—Deuteronomy 16:18-21:9
Judges and officers you shall appoint in all your gates,
tribe by tribe;
and they shall judge the people with true justice.

According to the commentaries of both Rabbi Ishmael and Simeon ben Yoḥai, Moses offered his life for the sake of the Torah, Israel, and justice. Consequently, each takes his name: Moses' law, Moses' people, Moses' appointed judges.

There is tension between the authority of law, divine or human, and the sovereignty of the self, if not the soul. Heaven requires, while the earth cries out.

The day after Moses slew an Egyptian for beating an Israelite, he tried to stop a fight between two Hebrews.

The aggressor asked, "Who made you a judge over us? would you kill me as you did the Egyptian?"[a]

And Moses, who had not yet met with the burning bush but now knew that no thing was hidden, fled.

On the last day of his life, Moses instructed Israel concerning the conduct of judges, officials and priests, of prophets and witnesses, and of kings, in the land God promised them. His precepts are not about individual satisfaction, mixed emotions, mitigation or appeal. These commandments begin in grievance, and use punishment to deter individual aggression and public disorder. Punishment, Maimonides argues, is a mercy. Without it, Israel would be governed by individual cruelty amid civic ruin.[303]

---

a. Exodus 2:14

Traditionally, a man who violates an easy precept will, in the end, violate a grave one.[304]

Thus, for the one who does not love his neighbor as himself, Moses taught that he will come to hate his brother, to take vengeance, or bear a grudge. His brother may not live with him,[a] lest blood be shed, or he lie in ambush for his neighbor, rise up against him, and strike him dead.

For the person who kills unintentionally, Moses established cities of refuge from vengeance—an institutional form of pity.

For those who commit idolatry and who kill for hatred, the law calls for stoning and blood.

As for the false witness, as he schemed to do against his fellow, do to him.

Show no pity: life for life, eye for eye, tooth for tooth, hand for hand, foot for foot.

Next, Moses speaks of war, which has method, but no law or truth.

When Israel takes the field against her enemies, a priest accompanies the Ark anointed for battle. He approaches and speaks to the people in the holy tongue, saying, "Hear, O Israel: Let not your heart faint at neighing horses, clash of swords and shields, the trumpets' blast, the battle cries."

Moses set rules of conduct toward the cities Israel would encounter in the land they would inherit:

Spare those cities that submit—they will pay tribute.

If distant cities on the way offer battle, kill all the men, but spare the women, children, and cattle—they are yours.

In the cities of the promised land, destroy everything that breathes—but spare the trees.

---

a. Leviticus 19:17-18; 36:22

The chapter on judges caps the prospect of annihilated cities with the process due innocent blood.

What justice can be done for a body found in an open field, murdered by an unknown hand?

The judges and elders of the town nearest the corpse must take a heifer which has never known work and lead it to an untilled valley. There, the elders must strike off the heifer's neck. The priests then approach, as the elders wash their hands over the beheaded heifer and say:

"Our hands have not shed this blood, nor have our eyes seen it.

"Forgive thy people Israel, O LORD, and suffer not innocent blood to remain in the midst of thy people."

The blood will be forgiven, Moses concludes, "when you do that which is right in the eyes of the LORD."

Solomon the Preacher knew seventy-two languages and understood the speech of animals.

He said of laughter, "It is mad."[a]

Abba bar Kahana commented, "With grief."

Rabbi Aḥa rendered Solomon's wisdom as, "I said of that which is punishable: It is radiant."

King Solomon was drawn to the glamor of things which Moses' justice taught are punishable. He multiplied wives, collected horses, amassed silver and gold.

"I broke the law," the king admitted,
"yet my offenses blazed with splendor."[305]

Solomon's father David held himself otherwise:
"As for me, I shall behold Thy face in kindness."

And Isaiah the consoler promised:

---

a. Ecclesiastes 2:2

"The glory of the LORD shall be revealed,

and all flesh will see it together."[a]

A midrash wonders, "All? No difference between the righteous and the wicked?"

And answers, "The wicked will know whom they vexed, while the righteous will know for whom they labored."

Another interprets the Psalmist's hope for himself as: "I shall behold your presence in justice."

Because the wicked prosper in this world even though they deny the Creator, and because the righteous suffer, even though they are willing to die for the Name, David said,

"I will not be among those who vex,

but of those who labor in the Law, where it is written:

'Justice, justice shalt thou follow.'"[306]

The Talmud explains: The first mention of justice refers to decisions based on strict law; the second refers to compromises.[307]

One day, Simeon the son of Yoḥai stepped outside and saw only dark. The world's light was sealed up.

His son Eleazar said: "Let's ask the holy One why such gloom."

The two set off, and found an angel, a tall mountain, shooting thirty flames of fire from its mouth.

Rabbi Simeon demanded: "What are you about?"

The mountain answered: "There are not thirty righteous men in this generation, so I am about to destroy the world."

The rabbi told the angel: "Go, please, tell the One that the son of Yoḥai lives here."

The angel went. He said to God: "Maker of the universe,

---

a. Isaiah 40:5

you already know what ben Yoḥai said to me."

And God said: "Go. Destroy the world. Pay no mind to Simeon ben Yoḥai."

The angel returned, but Simeon stopped him, saying:

"Mind, or I will keep you out of heaven and chain you beside Uzza and Azazel in the mountains of darkness.

"Go. Tell the holy One that if there be not thirty, or twenty, or even ten righteous men alive, yet there be two: myself and my son.

"Moses has written: 'One witness shall not rise up against a man for any sin. At the mouth of two witnesses, or of three, shall a matter, be established.' And matter, the word, means the world, since by the word of the LORD were the heavens made.[a]

"And if there be not two righteous men, there is at least one, myself. For the righteous man is the foundation of the world."[b]

A heavenly voice was heard:

"Light is your portion, Rabbi Simeon.

"The LORD makes a decree above,

and you annul it in the world below.[308]

"He fulfills the desire of those who fear Him;

hears their cry, and saves them."[c]

---

a. Psalm 33:6
b. Proverbs 10:25
c. Psalm 145:19

WHEN YOU GO OUT

CAN ONE KNOWINGLY FORGET?

KI TETSE'/כי־תצא—Deuteronomy 21:10-25:19
When you go out to battle against your enemies,
and the LORD your God delivers them into your hands,
and you carry them away captive.

Fretful Moses devotes one-hundred-ten verses to an anthology governing needs and urges Israel may encounter when they go out into the land across Jordan without him.

The Lawgiver prescribes conduct with desirable captive women, outlines a man's responsibilities towards his wives and children, defines the treatment due a stubborn, rebellious son and an executed person's corpse.

The chapter commands respect for property, abhors cross-dressing, protects mother birds, requires parapets on new-built houses, forbids the mixing of seeds, or of animals yoked to the plow, or of wool and linen in the same garment, and details the proceedings for impugned virginity, rape, adultery, seduction, a son who takes his father's wife or uncovers his father's skirt.

Moses excludes from the congregation those with crushed testicles, bastards, incestuous issue, Ammonites and Moabites, though not Edomites and Egyptians.

The Law requires that Israelite troops keep spades to dig latrines. More statutes shelter escaped slaves, abominate harlots and sodomites, forbid lending at interest to brethren, and vowing vows.

This portion also conveys rules for divorce, remarriage and first marriage, explains that each person is punished for his own sins not for those of his family, numbers the lashes given the wicked, provides for the poor and strangers, explicates the family's duty to the childless widow, the treatment of a wife who aids her husband in a fight, requires one keep just weights and measures, and concludes with the command to

"Remember what Amalek did to you by the way, as you went out from Egypt; how he met you by the way and cut off your extremities, all that were enfeebled in your rear, when you were faint and weary; and he feared not God.

"Therefore it shall be that you blot out remembrance of Amalek from under heaven; thou shalt not forget."

One rabbi taught that, after forty years, Moses actually wanted to ask Israel, "Do you remember when you said in the Wilderness, 'Is the LORD among us, or not?'" But rather than shame them, Moses taught the People the story of Amalek, so they would understand what came before.

Israel objected: "God commanded us to 'Remember the Sabbath day, to keep it holy.' But He also told us to 'Remember what Amalek did to you.'

"How can both commands be fulfilled?"

Moses answered "The cup of wine is not the cup of vinegar. The first remember is to observe and sanctify; that other remember is to destroy and cut off all the seed."

Israel forgot to utterly destroy Amalek but, through Samuel, God did not forget.[309]

As Rabbi Eliezer told it, the LORD took an oath upon His throne that under the whole heaven there should be left neither sprig nor sprout, so no one could even say:

"This tree is Amalek's;

"This camel, Amalek's;

"This ewe."[310]

There is no sleep in heaven, and no sitting.

When the prophets wept and sang, "If I forget thee O Jerusalem," they used the singular because the One, called "I," spoke through them, singing: "You weep, I weep with you."

By the rivers of Babylon, where they sat down, the singers wept, not because they remembered Zion, but because of the One who dwelt there.

They cried out, "Remember, LORD,[a] if not for our sake then for Your own."

God asked, "What thing shall I remember? I do not forget. Do you remember what Amalek did when you went out of Egypt? One who forgets to take care of himself ought not ask another to remember for him."[311]

Exactly what did Amalek do?

According to many rabbis, when Amalekites captured a lagging Israelite or one who went out to use a latrine by the way, they would cut off the circumcised organ from their living prisoner, fling it heavenwards, and taunt God with the offering:

"Is this what you have chosen? Take it."

Rabbi Levi detected an allusion to that taunt in the statute where, when two men struggle and the wife of one delivers her husband from his enemy by seizing his opponent's genitals, you must cut off her hand without pity. These verses are followed by God's command to remember what Amalek had done.

Berekiah replied to that imperative:

"You say to us, 'Remember.' You, too, should remember that we frequently forget.

"But, given that with You there's no forgetting, it's better You remember what Amalek has done to You."

---

a. Psalm 137

After Saul captured the Amalekite king Agag, Samuel demanded that the king be brought before him. Agag came with faltering steps, and murmured, "Ah, bitter death is at hand."[a]

With a sword, Samuel hewed olive-sized pieces of flesh from Agag and fed them to ostriches. Next, the priest, judge and prophet drove four stakes into the ground and bound the Amalekite to them, then cut off Agag's member, and had him torn apart.

Rav Kahana commented that, when a man has injured his fellow, the bitter memory never departs from the injured heart.[312]

At harvest time, a man forgot a sheaf of grain in his field.

He told his son: "Go, thank God on my behalf by giving one bullock as a burnt sacrifice and another as a peace offering, as the Torah instructs."

The son asked: "Father, why do you rejoice at the performance of this teaching more than any other?"

The man replied: "All the other Torah commandments can be performed consciously, but the statute that assigns forgotten sheaves to the poor cannot."

Can one knowingly forget?[313]

A psalm attributed to Moses[b] begins:
"Live sheltered by the shadow of the highest
    Mountain and remember
    When you walked through quicksand,
Plagues passed over others' doorsills in the dark,
Days when arrow swarms pursued and thousands fell
    Around you, and you stood, unmarked."

---

a. 1Samuel 15:32
b. Psalm 91

The Psalmist further counsels that you
"Not fear night's terror, nor the shaft of day,
  the plague that walks in darkness,
  nor destruction that swells up at noon."
In rabbinic tradition, these verses refer to the demon Bitter
Destruction. Covered with scales and shaggy hair, the demon
glares with one eye in the middle of his heart, and rolls like a
ball. He has no power if the shade remains cool while the sun is
hot, but Destruction prevails when it's hot in the shade and the
sun, in blazing summer.

From the seventeenth of Tammuz (when Babylon's armies
breached the walls of Jerusalem) to the Ninth of Av (when the
Temple fell), Bitter Destruction ranges from the fourth until the
ninth hour of daylight. All who see him fall upon their face.
Hezekiah saw him and collapsed. Phinehas the Priest the son of
Hama knew of a man who saw the demon, fell flat upon his
face, and became an epileptic.

Samuel the son of Rabbi Isaac advised that, during the
three weeks of mourning for the fall of David's city, teachers
should send their charges home before the heat of the day.
Rabbi Yoḥanan instructed schoolmasters that, when Bitter
Destruction walks abroad, you'd best not strike the children.[314]

WHEN YOU COME

AN ANTHOLOGY OF BLESSINGS IN TWELVE VERSES AND OF CURSES
IN FIFTY-FOUR VERSES, WITHOUT CONSOLATIONS

KI TAVO'/כי־תבוא—Deuteronomy 26:1-29:8
And it shall be, when you come into the land.

Moses taught: When you, Israel, come into the land flowing
with milk and honey, set up twelve stones covered with plaster,
and write upon the stones all the words of this law very plainly.

The twelve tribes will stand—six tribes on Mt. Gerizim to
bless the people, and six on Mt. Eval for the curse—while the
Levites raise their voice and say to every man of Israel[315] twelve
curses, for those who violate these commandments.

And after each curse, all the people shall say, "Amen."

According to Rashi, "plainly" means "in seventy
languages."

Rabbi Yoḥanan said that, while giving the Torah at Mt.
Sinai, God's voice split into seventy different voices, one for
each of the seventy languages, so all the nations could hear in
their native tongues. And when they did, they died of fright; but
Israel heard and was unharmed.[316]

In *Brown-Driver-Briggs Hebrew and English Lexicon,* אָרַר/arar
[curse] occupies slightly over half a column; בָּרַךְ/barakh [bless]
fills almost two columns. The fifth definition of "bless" is:
"antithetical, meaning curse, a blessing overdone and so really a
curse as in vulgar English."

Such a blessing is spoken in Psalms:
"For the wicked boasts of his hearts desire,
      and blesses the covetous, whom the LORD abhors."[a]

---

a. Psalm 10:3

This "bless" is also found four times in the book of Job:[a]

when Job said, "It may be that my sons have sinned, and cursed God in their hearts;"

when Satan said (to God, twice), "But put forth thine hand now, and he will curse thee to thy face;"

and when Job's wife said to him "Curse God, and die."

In Genesis, "curse" [אָרַר/arar] is first addressed to the serpent, "Because thou hast done this, thou art cursed above all cattle, and above every beast of the field; upon thy belly shalt thou go, and dust shalt thou eat all the days of thy life;"

and next, when God says to Adam, "Because thou hast hearkened unto the voice of thy wife, and hast eaten of the tree, of which I commanded thee, saying, 'Thou shalt not eat of it:' cursed is the ground for thy sake; in sorrow shalt thou eat of it all the days of thy life, till thou return unto the ground; for out of it wast thou taken: for dust thou art, and unto dust shalt thou return."[b]

Rabbi Eliezer taught that the LORD God's judgment upon the serpent, Eve, and Adam, consisted of nine curses and death.

But, Rabbi Ishmael observed, unlike His creatures, the Creator heals with the thing with which he smites. "Might this," the rabbi asked, "include the sword God placed at the east of Eden, a flaming sword which turned every way, to keep the way of the tree of life?"

God blessed the fifth, sixth, and seventh days of Creation:

First, he blessed the creatures of the waters and the air; then man, created in his own image, male and female; and finally, the Sabbath, the seventh day, because He rested.

a. Job 1:5; 1:11; 2:5; 2:9
b. Genesis 3:8-24

Noah recited the first blessing in the form בָּרוּךְ/barukh [bless, or blessed be].[a]

After the flood, Noah planted a vineyard, and made wine, and drank it. Drunk, he slept uncovered in his tent. When he awoke, the patriarch learned that Ham, the middle son, had seen his father naked, and told his brothers. First Noah cursed Ham. Then he blessed the LORD God of Shem, who (with his brother Japheth) had averted his gaze, and covered their father's nakedness with a cloak.

Cursed for revealing, blessed for concealing.

Rabbi Isaac thought blessing is possible only in that which is hidden from the eye.

Of the blessings promised Israel if they listen to God's voice and keep his laws, the school of Ishmael advised, "Pray first for a blessing on the work of your hands, then pray that the blessing be transferred to the work as it is measured.

"If you measure first, then pray, it is prayer in vain. Blessings cannot be found in anything already weighed, measured, or counted, but only in what is out of sight."

Moses cautioned every individual who would break the commandments written on stone with twelve curses in twelve verses. He then pronounced six blessings and six curses upon all Israel.

The promised blessings—"if you heed God's voice"—fill twelve verses.

The consequent curses—"if you do not hearken to the voice"—take fifty-four verses to be told.

The companions of Simeon ben Yoḥai were puzzled:[317]

---

a. Genesis 9:26

"The curses in Leviticus[a] refer to the first Temple, and the curses in Deuteronomy refer to the second Temple, the time of our exile.

"The Book of Priests contains assurances and an expression of God's love for Israel. But the curses in the Book of Admonitions contain no assurances, no consolation."

They sent a messenger dove to Rabbi Simeon, who had fled to the desert and hidden away in a cave with his son Eleazar. Simeon took the band from the dove's leg and read it, was bewildered, and wept.

Then Elijah came down from Heaven to the mouth of the cave, and brought Simeon this answer:

"Leviticus' curses have thirty-two verses:
the number of paths of wisdom in the hidden Torah.

"Deuteronomy's curses are fifty-four[318] verses:
the number of sections comprising the Five Books.

"At Solomon's Temple, Israel strayed from the hidden paths of the secret Torah, and their sins were revealed with consolations and assurances.

"At the second Temple, Israel transgressed against the revealed Torah, so their sin is hidden with their consolations.

"The holy One's great anger arouses mercy—open curses concealing blessings, curses made in love.

"Such is not the case with curses spoken in strict judgment."

Simeon asked, "Where is Israel's redemption revealed in these curses?"

Elijah told him, "Look, examine the most evil place. There you will find it."

Simeon looked in the darkest place and found:

---

a. Leviticus 26:14-44

"Your life will hang in doubt before you, and you will fear night and day, and you will have no assurance of your life."

Rabbi Hananiah said, "He who takes the words of the Torah to heart will be relieved of anxieties. But he who does not will be burdened by fears, as our teacher Moses wrote:

"'They shall serve as signs and proofs against you and your offspring for all time.

"'Because you would not serve the LORD your God in joy and gladness over the abundance of everything, you shall serve—hungry, thirsty, naked, lacking everything—the enemies whom the LORD will let loose against you.'"

Rabbi Judah asked, "Where do we learn that song is indispensable?"

Mattenah answered, "From the verse 'Because you did not serve with joy.'

"Which service is with joyful gladdened heart?

"Song."[319]

My heart danced when they said, Go in.
I stood inside the doorway to Jerusalem:
Jerusalem, the city of the LORD of all

Creation, ruler of the law, of people
Speaking heart to heart, where dream, word, thought,
Justice, judgment, thanks, and praise

Agree, where meeting, people talk
About Jerusalem, and talking sing of peace,
    Their only greeting.[a]

---

a. Psalm 122

And what is service lacking everything?
Ammi said, "This means with neither lamp nor table."
Hisda said, "Without a wife."
The blind Rabbi Sheshet said, "Without an attendant."
Rabbi Naḥman said, "Without knowledge."
Other sages taught, "Without salt or fat."
Abbaye said, "We have a tradition that only he who lacks knowledge is poor."

Judah Halevi wrote: "In order to be heard, a prayer must be recited for a multitude, or in a multitude, or for an individual who could take the place of a multitude.
"None such, however, is to be found in our age."[320]

A scholar at his desk at midnight
Looked up from his book, beyond the lamplight,
Into a socked-in yard where gray wisps swirled
Between clotheslines, and said:
Blessed be the creator of this world.[a]

---

a. Psalm 134

YOU STAND

ON THIS DAY, IN THE HARD PLACE, WITH HOPE FOR SOME
AND TRIALS FOR OTHERS

NITSAVIM/נצבים—Deuteronomy 29:9-30:20
You stand this day all of you before the LORD your God...

When we returned from far away
Our home looked as it looks in dreams:
The sun shines, gates swing
Open of themselves, and someone
Sings a song we had forgotten
As we now remember laughter.
Then strangers said, Great things
Were done for them.
        The LORD
Did great things for us then. A good.
But you must do great things again,
Because we live with heaviness
And twist and scatter like a river
Delta bogged in marsh and reeds.
We started sadly so we'd end up
Smiling, for anyone begins, sows
Seed with tears to reap his own,
The happy harvest, no?[a]

When Israel received the Law at Sinai, prophets of every generation heard what they would prophesy.

When Moses said, "one who stands here this day before the LORD our God, and also those not here with us this day"—he was speaking to the souls not yet created.

Waiting, each received a share of Torah.

---

a. Psalm 126

Where is that share? "Not in heaven,"
Moses said to those standing before him;
    "Do not say another Moses will arise
and bring another Torah, for I say:
No part of Torah has remained in heaven."

Scripture makes the ear to hear what it can hear, as best it can, on earth.[321]

Rabbi Eliezer heard the LORD Of Hosts say: "I have set before you life and good, and death and evil. Look! I have given Israel two ways: one good, the other evil. The good is life, and evil, death. Elijah stands between them. When someone sets out on the way of good, Elijah cries out, 'Open up the gates, so that the righteous who keep truth may enter.'"[a]

Eliezer continued, "Good also takes two paths—one righteousness, one love. At that forking, Samuel appears and asks the stranger, 'Which path do you choose?'

"Whichever way I take, the other road seems better, but I call Heaven and earth to witness, that I give up neither righteousness nor love."[322]

In another legend, Eliezer the Great determined that a certain kind of oven could not be defiled.

The Sages rejected all his arguments, and ruled it unclean.

Then Eliezer said, "If the Law agrees with me, let this carob tree prove it."

The tree upped its roots and replanted itself in another place.

The Sages replied, "Law can't be proven from a carob tree."

---

a. Isaiah 26:2

So Eliezer said, "If I am correct, let this water channel demonstrate it."

And its waters flowed backward.

The Sages countered, "You can't adduce proof from a stream."

Again Eliezer pressed his suit, "If my decision is the right one, let the walls of this study house bear witness."

At this, the walls leaned and were about to topple.

But Rabbi Joshua rebuked the walls: "The wise dispute, and you interfere?"

And the walls neither fell, nor stood upright.

At last, Rabbi Eliezer told the Sages, "If the Law agrees with me, let it be ratified from heaven."

A heavenly voice was heard:

"Why do you deny Eliezer, with whom the Law always agrees?"

Rabbi Joshua demurred. "Torah is not in heaven.

In our disputes, we pay no attention to a voice from heaven."

Years later, Rabbi Nathan met Elijah and asked him, "What did God do in that moment?"

Elijah reported, "The Maker laughed, saying, 'My sons have defeated Me, My sons have defeated Me.'"

On New Year, all the living pass before the One, who opens up three books:

    one for the wholly righteous;

    one for the wholly wicked;

    and one for those in-between.

At this annual hearing,

    the righteous are inscribed and sealed in the book of life;

the wicked are entered in the book of death;
for everyone else, judgment is suspended for the Days of Awe.

The School of Shammai rules that, on Judgment Day, the righteous gain life in the world to come; the wicked are sealed forever in Gehenna; those mixed of good and evil also go down to the terrible place, but when they cry out in their suffering, they rise again.

The School of Hillel holds that He that abounds in grace inclines toward grace.

Whatever's held in store for us, the ten tribes
    are not destined to come back, because
The LORD cast them into another land,
        as on this day.
Akiba taught: "As this day goes and does not return,
    so they went and will not return."
But Eliezer understands "As on this day" to mean:
    "As day begins in darkness then lights up,
so their darkness will light up for them."
    So it goes in this world, and the other,
according to both Scripture and tradition.
    Making his case for hope, Saadia Gaon reasoned that,
"If what has happened in the past
    can be used as proof and an example,
then God will do for us in days to come
    twice two times better than He promised us.
"So Moses wrote: 'He will do you good
    and multiply you above your fathers.'
"Therefore," Saadia says, "don't entertain the thought
    that God is not aware of us,
        or that He does not deal fairly,

or that He is not compassionate,
or that He cannot help, or answer
prayer; nor is it proper to believe
He has forsaken us and cast us off."
In Saadia's opinion, God set limits on what is His alone,
  the mystery:[323] "One limit is repentance;
the other is determined by the end.
    "Whichever one comes first will bring redemption.
    "Therefore, if our repentance be complete,
no regard would be paid to the end.
    "Yet, should our repentance fail, we will have to wait
until the end, its punishments and trials.
    "This rule applies to all catastrophes,
in times of famine, war, and pestilence, which serve, we think,
as punishment for some, and trial for others.
    "If history is proof, or an example."

If history is proof or an example,
we stand in the hard place, inscribed and sealed.
    The statement "If I die" is never true.
Both truth and mystery require "when."
    Why do even sages talk this way?
One answered: "Before my time" is understood.
    No one expects to live forever.
Another said: It means, "If I should lose
  my self, my soul, my way while yet
alive...," but then the statement must
    be followed by a "then."
My thoughts grew tangled in the trees,
    the lime trees and the wind.
Perhaps the living part proclaims its rights

and—speaking for itself and not
the mortal part—must always be preferred
   in conversation. So I understood
The Book of Moses when he said, "Choose life."

HE WENT

ON MOSES'S 120ᵀᴴ BIRTHDAY, HE DIED UNDER PROTEST
AND SANG BY COMMAND

VA-YELEKH/וילך—Deuteronomy 31:1-31:30
Moses went and spoke these words to all Israel.

One midnight the Angel of Death met Simeon ben Ḥalafta on
the road.

Rabbi Simeon asked, "Who are you?"

The angel answered, "God's messenger."

Simeon, "Why do you look so strange?"

The angel answered, "I look this way because people say,
'I will do this and that,' and yet not one of them knows when he
will be summoned."

Simeon asked the messenger to reveal the time of his own
end.

Death said, "I have no dominion over such as you, because
God delights in your deeds, and grants the righteous extra
days."

Akiba raised his hand. "Enough! What does this story have
to do with anything? Moses kept the law, did works of charity,
yet in the end God said, 'The time draws near for you to die.'
So it follows: There is a time to be born, and a time to die."

From the first of Shvat to the sixth of Adar, over thirty-six days,
Moses explained the entire Torah.

On the sixth, God told Moses he was done.

On the seventh of Adar, Moses spoke these words to all
Israel: "One-hundred-twenty-years old am I today."

Moses said "today" to teach that he was born on the
seventh of Adar, and on the seventh he died.[324]

Rabbi Yannai clarified: "When Moses learned he was to

die, on that day he wrote thirteen scrolls of law—one for each of the twelve tribes, and one to be placed in the ark, as a master text.

"When the law was entirely completed, Moses gave it to the Levites and commanded them that, every seven years 'in the place God chooses, thou shalt read this law aloud before all Israel.' That way, the Talmud[325] explains, the men learn, the women hear, and the little ones earn a reward for those who bring them."

God said to Moses, "Behold, your days approach that you must die;" and said again, "Behold! you are about to sleep with your fathers, and this people will rise up and go astray."

Moses retorted,[326] "In the chapter called 'Because' I praised you with'"Behold!'[a] and you decree my death with the same word?"

God answered, "You praised me there, but when I sent you to deliver them from Egypt, you derided Israel and said, 'Behold! they will not believe me.'"[b]

Then Moses asked, "Have I broken any law punishable by death?"

God replied, "You die because Adam brought death into the world and I said: 'Behold! the man is become as one of us, to know.'"[c]

Maimonides deduced that providence constantly cares for an individual whose mind never turns away from God. Should one's thoughts sometimes turn to other things, providence withdraws during the time of distraction. Such a person is like a skillful scribe when he is not writing. On the other hand,

a. Deuteronomy 10:14
b. Exodus 4:1
c. Genesis 3:22

someone who never engages God with his intellect is like a person in darkness.

It follows that a mind free from distraction can never be afflicted with evil of any kind. Abandon God, however, and one's thoughts become a target for every evil that may befall. Torah provides the proof text:

"And I will hide My face from them,
and many evils and troubles will come upon them;
so that they say in that day:
'Are not these evils come because our God is not among us?'"

The philosopher stresses that, "We, who pay no mind, cause God to say: 'On that day I will hide my face;'" and concludes: "How terrible this threat."[327]

On that day, God commanded Moses: "Write this song, and teach it, and put it in their mouths as a witness against Israel."

So Moses wrote:
"Give ear, O ye heavens, and I will speak;
    and hear, O earth, the words of my mouth."

Psalm 78, attributed to the musician Asaph, begins
"Give ear, O my people, to my teaching;
    incline your ears to the words of my mouth."

The midrash comments: "The One made a covenant with Israel only for the sake of the Torah, so that it be remembered and recited by their children. Lest someone claim that the Psalms of David are not law, the song says: 'Give ear to my Torah.' Revelations, riddles and parables—the Books of the Prophets and the Writings—are also Torah."

God directed the Son of man to put forth a riddle and speak a parable.[a] Solomon likewise enjoined his son to understand a

---

a. Ezekiel 17:2

proverb, and the interpretation; the words of the wise, and their dark sayings.[a]

Asaph's psalm is a maschil, meaning it requires further explanation.

When the musician opened his mouth with a parable, and uttered dark sayings about past days, someone asked, "How do you know about what you sing? Have you seen it?"

Asaph answered, "I know that which we have heard."

About "this song."

Moses recited three of the ten songs in the Torah: the song beside the Red Sea; the song the tribes sang at the well; and lastly, "when Moses made an end of writing the words of this law in a book, until they were finished, Moses spoke in the ears of all Israel the words of this song until they were ended."

How can this book of Torah be complete, and at the same time record that Moses died?

The book does not say Moses wrote these words in the order they appear when finished.

Simeon ben Yoḥai told Rabbi Judah that, "up to the passage 'So Moses died,'[b] the holy One dictated and Moses repeated aloud as he wrote; but from here on, the One dictated and Moses, without speaking, wrote down God's words with tears in his eyes."[328]

In the tractate *Decisions*, the Sages of Palestine place the systematic arranger of traditions above the reasoner who asks and answers questions.[329]

---

a. Proverbs 1:6
b. Deuteronomy 34:5

GIVE EAR!

MOSES'S LAST DISPUTE WITH GOD, AND THAT LONG SPEECH
CALLED A SONG

HAʿAZINU/הַאֲזִינוּ—Deuteronomy 32:1-52
Give ear, you heavens, and I will speak;
and let the earth hear the words of my mouth.

Before he sang his last, his second song, Moses promised Israel
that the Torah would neither leave them nor be lost.[a]

Some say the Torah was lost after the fall of the first
Temple, but that Ezra the scribe returned to Jerusalem from
Babylon, and wrote it down from memory.[b] The only words
Ezra could not recall open a verse from Solomon's Song.[c]
Perplexed, the scribe asked a random passerby, "Do you know
how the verse begins that ends "the chariots of my generous
nation?"

The unlearned Jew answered, "I don't know,"—because he
didn't—which reminded Ezra that the verse begins "I did not
know."[330]

Akiba said to Rabbi Yoḥanan, "Let's recite 'The Song of
Songs,' the best of songs, songs for the One who left a remnant
of us in this world."

The two agreed, "Let us sing many songs before Him.
Where Moses' songs glorify the Maker, Solomon's God praises
people, crooning:

'Behold, you are fair, my love, you are fair;'
and Israel sings back:

'Behold, beloved, you are fair, and please me'[d]—
the song of songs, a doubled song, an echo mirror."

---

a. Deuteronomy 31:21
b. Ezra 7:1-10
c. Song of Songs 6:12
d. Song of Songs 1:15-16

Rabbi Levi found this interpretation far too literary: "God holds two matters in one hand. For Job, these are the soul of every living thing[a], and judgment. For Moses, they are commandment and song: His right hand holds a fiery law[b] and righteousness."[c] [331]

Moses composed eleven psalms, numbers 90 through 100. They appear in the Books of David, not in the Books of Moses because, Levi contends, Moses' books are words of Torah and David's, words of prophecy.[332]

Rashi adds that the teacher's psalms correspond to those blessings on the eleven tribes Moses spoke before he died.[d]

In the last hour of his life, Moses said to God, "If You do not bring me into the Land of Israel, then leave me in this world so I may not die."

God answered, "How can I let you live? Would you falsify the Torah, where you wrote: 'None can deliver out of My hand?'"

Moses begged, "Let my soul become like a beast of the field that eats grass and drinks water and enjoys the world."

God answered, "No more talk. Just song."

Then Moses took a scroll, inscribed the Name on it and "These, the words, the Book of Song," when his last moment came.

As Moses' soul grappled with death, he spoke to her:
"My soul, do you think this angel can rule over you?
Have you seen people weeping, and wept too?

a. Job 12:10
b. Deuteronomy 33:2
c. Psalm 98
d. Deuteronomy 33

Do you fear being thrust into the formless void?"
His soul replied: "Surely God will not permit it, for you sang,
  'You have delivered my soul from death,
    my eyes from tears, my feet from stumbling.'"
Moses asked: "Where will you go?"
She answered: "I will walk before the LORD
  in the lands of the living."
And Moses said: "Return, my soul, to rest."[a] [333]

Isaiah prophesied, "And it will come to pass that,
  before they call, I will answer,
  and while they are still speaking, I will hear.[b]
    Seek the One when He can be found;
    call on Him when He is near."[c]
David counseled, "Seek His presence constantly."[d]
Moses revealed: "See now that I, I, am He,
  no god beside Me."[334]

"And so," Tanḥuma summarized, "He appears, and He cannot be seen; sometimes He listens, sometimes, answers; at times He is silent, near, or far."[335]

After Moses spoke all the words of this song in the ears of the people, he made an end, and said, "Take to heart all these words which I testify among you today, all the words of this law, because it is no empty thing for you, because it is your life."

Akiba explains that, "If a thing is empty, it is so on your account, because you don't know how to understand what's said, or written, be the matter song or law.

---

a. Psalm 96:8
b. Isaiah 65:24
c. Isaiah 55:6
d. 1Chronicles 16:11

"In the beginning, Adam was formed from the dust, and Eve from Adam. From then to now, we are made in our own image, neither man without woman nor woman without man, nor both of them without the Source."[336]

Simeon ben Yoḥai questioned his companions. "How long shall we read these words?

"Look, we teach the Unpronounceable, and we know matters; we have shown things unknown to those before us.

"From here on, all these words—put them aside."

Rabbi Isaac responded: "Moses revealed all these words only on the very day he died, and even then he did not speak, until God told him 'Now, write down this song'[a] and first addressed the heavens, then Israel."

Yose begged to differ: "This song? That speech is called a song?"

Isaac answered: "Certainly. Just like psalms engendered by the heart from One above in one below, these words were inspired. Moses spoke a song.

"When Moses said 'Give ear,' Creation trembled, and a voice asked: 'Moses, Moses, why this detonation?' Then Moses wrote, 'The name of the LORD I call.'

"All heaven and earth fell silent, and listened to his words."[337]

Later, in Psalms and in the Prophets, David sang:
>Silence is praise.[b]
Because I just believed that I could
>Change my heart,
Not how the other people were,
>Nor when I came

a. Deuteronomy 31:19
b. Psalm 65:1

Or go from here, I didn't snarl
    Hope and fear, bound
To needless need and anger, greed,
    The appetites
That grow the more they feed.

There is a light. By its beams
    I pass through crowds
Across the barricades, past rock,
    Up gravel paths
With switchbacks to an overlook,
    Commanding
The high ground, which gently
    Slopes away,
Where I can see whole generations
    Turn to dust
Who have tormented me,
    And hear their cries
But need not heed them. Rumors
    Of the Lord
Bestow more power than poetry
    Sung by an unbeliever,
And I have found such temper
    In those judgments
I have left to time, as praise gives
    To the prayer,
Ruler over first myself,
    Then blessings.[a]
Or
    Be silent, and I will be silent.

---

a. Psalm 18, 2Samuel 22, Psalm 37

AND THIS, THE BLESSING

CELEBRATES THE END OF THE TORAH SCROLL,
AND THE BEGINNING OF THE NEW READING CYCLE

VE-ZO'T HA-BERAKHAH/וזאת הברכה—Deuteronomy 33:1-34:12
And this, the blessing wherewith Moses the man of God
blessed the children of Israel before his death.

A lion, a dog, and an Ethiopian flea found themselves in the
same place. The lion crouched to set upon the dog, but when he
saw the flea he backed down. The flea is the lion's bane, while
the dog scratches the flea.[338]

"Ah," said Rabbi Akiba: "How various your works, O
LORD. The earth is full of Your creation."[a]

Bless the pitcher of the sky's light tent,
(Winds are tentpoles, clouds stays)
Who draws the curtains, sends out messengers:
Old stars chilling distances;
The rising sun burns puddles hung with rope
Mists on the changing earth.
Bless the layer of the rock foundation,
Raiser of the great divides,
Where rivers fork to east or west, in beds,
And find sea level in the end,
And rise again. Fresh springs, rock wells quench
All thirsts that walk, or fly, or set
Seed, bud, green up and flower fruit: wine
Grapes to ease the heart; fat olives,
Herbs and cereal grasses for baked bread.
Sap rises in the junipers
Of Lebanon: storks nest there. In cliff clefts

---

a. Psalm 104:24

Mountain goats hopscotch and butt.
The moon marks fallow plowing sowing harvest
Seasons, and the sun sets. Nights,
Horned owls hunt for mice, and lions roar
At starlight for large prey. Dawn,
Raptors flap or slip back to the den,
Leaving day work to the human
Makers of their own invented prizes.
Ocean—broad and sometimes taller
Than the headland, silver shadow creatures
Glide through transparent density,
Slip underneath the keel like lives of people
Only known as chthonic rumor—
Floats Leviathan, fed on krill and plankton,
The largest on the smallest, full.
Creation grazes from your open hand:
God, never turn away.
Without the breath, all's clay, and dead.
Love answers fear. Earth's
Greater than what's known. What's known
Exceeds what's said.
So touch the mountains with your smoking finger.
I'll chant praises of my being
Here long as I can. The ignorant,
Their darkness, disappear.[a]

a. Psalm 104

OR THIS:

The *Perek Shirah*, an ancient Hebrew poem of indeterminate origin, places a biblical or rabbinic passage in the mouth of each of the eighty-four parts of creation as recounted in Genesis, from Heaven to dogs.

Some commentaries say King David wrote the poem. In the tenth through the sixteenth century, Ashkenazic and Sephardic versions served as a portable liturgy. One tradition states in the name of Yehudah the Prince that immersion in the *Perek Shirah* delivers the student from the Evil Impulse, and prolongs life.

"And," Rabbi Eliezer the Great promises, "Anyone who recites even part of *A Chapter of Song* in this world sings it with Moses in the world to come."

The story goes that David,
    when his Psalms were done
grew proud and, looking at the sky, said:
    "What in all Creation's
    sung more songs than I?"
A bullfrog happened by, and warned him:
    "David, don't be so puffed-up.
    "At dusk I croak ten times more songs,
more praises than you twanged in your whole life.
More, each grunt of mine sounds like 3,000 meanings,
    each one a blessing.
"You feed the heron wading in still water?
    "Do you hear what you can see?
    "Then help me finish singing."
Eighty-four short solos later,

once the dog was done,
a young man fasted for six days, objecting:
    "Dogs eat dung. They get to sing?"
An angel answered: "Eat.
    "No dog bared fangs at Moses
when he led you out of Egypt.
    "Dog dung tans the hides
our scrolls are written on.
    "Dogs earned their song.
    "You, watch your tongue."

Sources

Agnon, S. Y., *Days of Awe*, Schocken Books
    Present at Sinai, Jewish Publication Society

Ancient Near Eastern Texts Relating to the Old Testament, Third Edition with Supplement, ed. James B. Pritchard, Princeton University Press [ANET]

Artemidorus, *Interpretation of Dreams: Oneirocritica*, Original Books

The Babylonian Talmud: Volume 1-10, tr. Michael Rodkinson, The Talmud Society

Babylonian Talmud, Soncino Press Online Edition

ben HaRambam, Rabbi Avraham, *The Guide to Serving God*, Feldheim

Bialik, Chaim/Haim/Hayyim Nahman
    Selected Poems Of C.N. Bialik, tr. David Aberbach, Overlook
    Songs from Bialik: Selected Poems of Hayim Nahman Bialik, tr. Atar Hadari, Syracuse University Press
    Revealment and Concealment: Five Essays, Ibis Editions

Bialik, Hayyim Nahman, and Rawnitzky, Y. H., *The Book of Legends/ Sefer Ha-Aggadah: Legends from the Talmud and Midrash*, Schocken

The Bible: Authorized King James Version with Apocrypha, Oxford University Press

Biblia Hebraica: Stuttgartensia

Blake, William
    The Early Illuminated Books: All Religions Are One/There Is No Natural Religion/the Book of Thel/the Marriage of Heaven and Hell/ Visions of the Daughters of Albion, Princeton University Press
    The Complete Writings of William Blake with Variant Reading, Oxford University Press

Blenkinsopp, Joseph
  Isaiah 1-39, Anchor Bible 19
  Isaiah 40-55, Anchor Bible 19A
  Isaiah 56-66 Anchor Bible 19B, Doubleday

Boccaccio, Giovanni, *Genealogy of the Pagan Gods, volume I, Books I-IV*, tr. Jon Solomon, Harvard University Press

Brillat-Savarin, Jean Anthelme, *The Physiology of Taste*, tr. M. F. K. Fisher, Vintage Books

Brown-Driver-Briggs, *Hebrew and English Lexicon,* Hendrickson Publishers

Budge, E. A. Wallis, *Amulets and Superstitions: The Original Texts With Translations and Descriptions...*, Dover Books

Einstein, Albert, *Relativity*, Methuen Publishing

Fox, Everett, *The Five Books of Moses: The Schocken Bible, Volume I*, Schocken Books

Freud, Sigmund, *The Interpretation of Dreams*, tr. A.A. Brill, MacMillan

Ginzberg, Louis, *The Legends of the Jews, Vol I-VII*, Jewish Publication Society

Greenberg, Moshe
  Ezekiel 1-20, Anchor Bible 22
  Ezekiel 21-37, Anchor Bible 22A, Doubleday

Halevi, Jehudah/Yehudah/Judah
  The Kuzari: an Argument for the Faith of Israel, tr. H. Hirschfeld, Schocken [Kuzari]
  The Kuzari: In Defense of the Despised Faith, tr. N. Daniel Korobkin, Feldheim

Halevi *(cont)*
   Selected Poems of Jehudah Halevi, tr. Nina Salaman, Jewish
Publication Society
   On the Sea, tr. Gabriel Levin, Ibis Editions
   Poems from the Diwan, tr. Gabriel Levin, Anvil Press

Hebrew-English Tanakh, Student Edition, Jewish Publication Society

Hertz, J. H., *The Pentateuch and Haftorahs: Hebrew Text English
Translation and Commentary,* Soncino Press

Hesiod, The Homeric Hymns, and Homerica, trans. H. G. Evelyn-
White, Loeb Classical Library, Harvard University Press

Ibn Chaviv, Rabbi Yaakov, *Ein Yaakov: The Ethical and Inspirational
Teachings of the Talmu*d, tr. Avraham Yaakov Finkel, Jason Aronson

Ibn Ezra, Abraham, *Twilight of a Golden Age: Selected Poems of
Abraham Ibn Ezra,* tr. Leon J. Weinberger, University of Alabama
Press

Ibn Gabirol, Solomon
   Ibn Gabirol, tr. Raphael Loewe, Grove Press
   Selected Poems of Solomon Ibn Gabirol, tr. Peter Cole, Princeton
University Press
   Selected Religious Poems of Solomon Ibn Gabirol, tr. Israel
Zangwill, Jewish Publication Society

Josephus, Flavius, *The Genuine Works of Flavius Josephus the Jewish
Historian,* tr. William Whiston, Walker

Judaism on Trial: Jewish-Christian Disputations in the Middle Ages,
ed. and tr. Hyam Maccoby, Littman Library of Jewish Civilization

Maimonides, Moses, *The Guide of the Perplexed,* tr. Shlomo Pines,
vols 1-2, University Of Chicago Press [Guide]

Mekhilta De-Rabbi Ishmael: A Critical Edition, in 2 volumes, tr J. Z. Lauterbach, Jewish Publication Society

Mekhilta De-Rabbi Shimon Bar Yoḥai, tr. W. D. Nelson, Jewish Publication Society

Midrash on Psalms, tr. Wm. G. Braude, Yale University Press

Midrash Rabbah, tr. Maurice Simon, Soncino Press

Midrash Tanchuma, tr. Avrohom Davis, Metsudah Publications

Milgrom, Jacob
    Leviticus 1-16, Anchor Bible 3, Doubleday
    Leviticus 17-22, Anchor Bible 3A
    Leviticus 23-27, Anchor Bible 3B, Yale University Press

Milton, John, *The Complete English Poetry of John Milton*, ed. J. T. Shawcross, New York University Press

Nehunya ben haKana, *The Bahir: A Translation and Commentary*, tr. Aryeh Kaplan, Jason Aronson

Nemoy, Leon, *Karaite Anthology*, Yale University Press

Nietzsche, Friedrich, *The Birth of Tragedy from the Spirit of Music*, tr. Francis Golffing, Doubleday Anchor

The Old Testament Pseudepigrapha, Volumes 1 & 2, ed. James H. Charlesworth, Doubleday

Ovid (Publius Ovidius Naso)
    Metamorphoses, tr. F. J.Miller, Heinemanns
    Shakespeare's Ovid, tr. Wm. Golding, Centaur Press

Patai, Raphael, *Gates to the Old City: A Book of Jewish Legends,* Jason Aronson Inc.

Pentateuch and Rashis Commentary: A Linear Translation Into English, tr. Abraham Ben Isaiah and Benjamin Sharfman, SS&R Publishing Company

Pesikta De-Rab Kahana, tr. Wm. G. Braude, Jewish Publication Society

Pesikta Rabbati: Homiletical Discourses for Festal Days and Special Sabbaths 1 & 2, tr. Wm. Braude, Yale University Press

Philo of Alexandria, *The Works of Philo*, tr. C. D. Yonge, Hendrickson Publishers

Pirkê de Rabbi Eliezer, tr. Gerald Friedlander, Intellectbooks

Plutarch
    Lives of Noble Grecians and Romans, tr. John Dryden, Modern Library
    Moralia, Volume V, Isis and Osiris. The E at Delphi. The Oracles at Delphi No Longer Given in Verse. The Obsolescence of Oracles, tr. F. C. Babbitt, Loeb Classical Library

Propp, William, *Exodus 1-18*, Anchor Bible 2; *Exodus 19-40*, Anchor Bible 2A, Doubleday

Rashi, *Rashis Commentary on Psalms*, tr. Mayer I. Gruber, Jewish Publication Society

Saadia Gaon: *The Book of Beliefs and Opinions*, tr. Samuel Rosenblatt, Yale University Press [Beliefs and Opinions]

Sarna, Nahum, *On the Book of Psalms,* Schocken

Seder Olam: The Rabbinic View of Biblical Chronology, tr. H. W. Guggenheimer, Jason Aronson Inc.

Seznec, Jean, *The Survival of the Pagan Gods*, tr. Barbara F. Sessions, Princeton University Press

Sun Tzu, *The Art of War*, trans S. B. Griffith, Buccaneer Books

Tanna Debe Eliyyahu: The Lore of the School of Elijah, tr. I.J. Kapstein, Jewish Publication Society
Tishby, Isaiah, *The Wisdom of the Zohar: An Anthology of Texts*, tr. David Goldstein, Littman Library of Jewish Civilization

Trachtenberg, Joshua, *Jewish Magic and Superstition: A Study in Folk Religion*, University of Pennsylvania Press

Vico, Giambattista, *The New Science*, ed. Bergin and Fisch, Cornell University Press

Wieder, Laurance
    Words to God's Music: A New Book of Psalms, Eerdmans
    The Last Century: New and Selected Poems, Picador Australia
    Perek Shirah:A Chapter of Song, A New Version, Omerta Publications

Wittgenstein, Ludwig, *Tractatus Logico-Philosophicus*, Routledge and Kegan Paul

Yemenite Midrash: Philosophical Commentaries on the Torah, ed. Y. Tzvi Langermann, HarperOne

Zacuto, Abraham, *The Book of Lineage*, tr. and ed. Israel Shamir, Zacuto Foundation

Zohar, tr. Maurice Simon, Soncino Press

Zohar: Pritzker Edition
    vols 1-9, tr. Daniel Matt
    vol. 10, tr. Nathan Wolski
    vol. 11, tr. Joel Hecker
    vol. 12, tr. Wolski and Hecker, Stanford University Press

Notes

Genesis

1. Kuzari, pp. 198-204
2. Midrash on Psalms 92
3. Naming the animals, God's grief, and Adam's dismay: Pesikta de-Rab Kahana, Piska 4, 15 and 24
4. The generation of the Flood: Genesis Rabbah 36.1, 4-7 and 34.11
5. Midrash on Psalms 34
6. Nimrod and the Tower: Pirkei de Rabbi Eliezer 24; Genesis Rabbah 38.1 and .8
7. Midrash on Psalms 2
8. Noah's circumcision, group three idolators, interpretation of David's prayer, and description of Babel's ruins: Midrash Tanḥuma, Noaḥ
9. Zohar 1:76b
10. Genesis Rabbah 61.16 and 95.3; Mteh 1:13
11. Zohar 1:77b-78a
12. Genesis Rabbah 38.13; Tanna Debe Eliyyahu, ER pp. 27-28
13. Pesikta Rabbati, Piska 33.3
14. Genesis Rabbah 31.11
15. Genesis Rabbah 46.3
16. Midrash Tanḥuma, Vayera
17. Guide I,2 and 4; II,6
18. Midrash he-Ḥefeṣ
19. BT, Shabbat, 55a
20. Guide III,24-25
21. Kuzari, pp. 282-3
22. Ein Yakov, Sanhedrin, pp. 639-40
23. Zohar, 1:120b
24. Satan, Abraham and Isaac: Midrash Tanḥuma, Vayera
25. Genesis Rabbah 55.8
26. Zohar, 1:103a
27. Genesis Rabbah 56.8
28. Book of Legends, 579:37
29. Sarah's death and burial: Genesis Rabbah 58.5; 58.2 and .4
30. Book of Legends, 448:432
31. Midrash on Psalms 90

32. Ein Yaakov
33. Midrash on Psalms 116
34. Genesis Rabbah 63.11-12
35. Legends of the Jews
36. Isaac's blindness, Jacob and Esau's blessing: Genesis Rabbah
    65.9-10, .21 and 67.2
37. Pesikta de-Rab Kahana, S1
38. Guide II,6
39. Genesis 28:10-19
40. Mekhilta de-Rabbi Shimon bar Yoḥai, 45.8
41. Zohar 1:167b; 1:166a
42. Pesikta Rabbati 3.4
43. Book of Legends, 49:83
44. Legends of the Jews
45. Pesikta de-Rab Kahana, 17.3
46. Midrash Tanḥuma, Mikkets
47. Zohar 1:193b; 1:199b
48. BT Chagigah 12a
49. Genesis Rabbah 42.1
50. Midrash Tanḥuma, Mikkets
51. Guide I,18; I,27
52. Genesis Rabbah 93.6, .4 and .9
53. Midrash Tanḥuma, Vayigash
54. Bahir, Part 1, 191
55. Pesikta Rabbati, 21.13, 21.12
56. Zohar 1:224a; 1:235a

Exodus

57. The names of Moses; and the mountain, the call and thorn bush:
    Exodus Rabbah 1.26, 2.4; Numbers Rabbah 1.7; Exodus Rabbah
    2.5 and .6
58. Exodus Rabbah 3.5-6
59. Kuzari, p. 202
60. Guide I,63
61. Exodus Rabbah 3.4
62. Mekhilta de-Rabbi Shimon bar Yoḥai 2.5.1
63. Pesikta Rabbati, 33.8

64. Exodus Rabbah 5.14
65. BT Sanhedrin 67b
66. Zohar, 2:23a
67. Rashi, Exodus
68. Zohar, 2:37a; 2:38b
69. Seder Olam
70. Israel emerges from the Red Sea and sings: Exodus Rabbah 23.7, 23.15; Mekhilta de-Rabbi Shimon bar Yoḥai 29.1.8-9; Mekhilta de-Rabbi Ishmael, Shirata 3; Exodus Rabbah 23.4
71. Rashi, Exodus
72. Zohar 2:54a, fn. 275
73. Mekhilta de-Rabbi Shimon bar Yoḥai 34.1-2.5; Mekhilta de-Rabbi Ishmael, Shirata 8; Rabbi Shimon 29.1.1-5
74. Pesikta Rabbati, 29/30A.3
75. Pesikta de-Rab Kahana 12.6
76. Mekhilta de-Rabbi Shimon bar Yoḥai 20.5.2
77. Midrash Tanḥuma, Yitro
78. Pirke de Rabbi Eliezer 31
79. Beit Aharon, found in Agnon, Present at Sinai
80. Zohar, 2:81b
81. Yalkut, Yitro; found in Book of Legends
82. Midrash Tanḥuma, Shemot
83. Mekhilta de-Rabbi Ishmael, Shirata 8
84. Guide II,33
85. Exodus Rabbah 28.6
86. Zohar, 2:83b
87. Zohar 2:206a-b (Tishby)
88. Sefer Eshkol, Laws of the Priestly Blessings, found in Agnon
89. Bahir, Part 1, 45
90. BT Shabbat 88a
91. Yalkut David, found in Present at Sinai
92. Mekhilta de-Rabbi Shimon bar Yoḥai 50:2:16
93. BT Berachoth 5a
94. Mekhilta de-Rabbi Shimon bar Yoḥai 49.5.13
95. Zohar, 2:99a
96. Pesikta de-Rab Kahana 10.9
97. Guide III,28
98. Book of Legends, 544:71

99. Bahir, Part 1, 97
100. The Tabernacle, work: Pesikta Rabbati, 20.4, 5.9
101. Rashi, Exodus
102. Cherubim: Zohar 2:277a-2:278b
103. BT Bava Batra 99a, found in Matt, Zohar 3:59a-b
104. Zohar 2:176a
105. Legends of the Jews
106. Anchor Bible, Exodus 19-40
107. BT, Yoma 73b; Sotah 36b
108. Zohar I, 231a-b; Zohar II, 229b-230a (Tishby)
109. Ein Yaakov
110. Book of Legends, 16:67
111. Zohar 2:234a-b
112. New Science, 447
113. Ein Yaakov
114. Maccoby, Judaism on Trial, p. 179
115. Zohar 2:188a
116. Rashi, Exodus
117. Book of Legends, 487:19
118. Yemenite Midrash, 12.29
119. Midrash Tanḥuma, Terumah
120. On the practical arts: Exodus Rabbah 50.1, 48.4 and .3, and 50.2
121. Exodus Rabbah 51.8
122. Book of Legends, 472:49
123. Kuzari, pp. 161-162
124. Seder Olam
125. Sirâj al-'Uqûl
126. Completing the work: Zohar 2:222b-223a; 2:241b; Zohar II, 148b-149a (Tishby); Zohar 2:241b
127. Guide I,64
128. Pesikta Rabbati, Piska 5.7

Leviticus

129. Pesikta de-Rab Kahana 6.3
130. Lamentations Rabbah 1:1
131. Tanna Debe Eliyyahu, EZ p. 173
132. Zohar 2:182a-b

133. Zohar IV (Soncino) Vayikra 25a-b
134. Pesikta Rabbati, Piska 23/24.1
135. Kuzari, 2:67-80 (Korobkin)
136. Tanna Debe Eliyyahu, ER p. 38
137. "The Verse," Paradise Lost
138. Zohar III, 28b-29a, Raya Mehemna (Tishby)
139. Yemenite Midrash 6.3 Nûr al-Ẓalâm
140. Pesikta de-Rab Kahana 6.3
141. Pesikta Rabbati 48.3
142. BT Kiddushin: 2a-40b, found in Kuzari, p. 165
143. Sifra
144. Pesikta de-Rab Kahana 4.5
145. Zohar 3:14a
146. Guide III,33
147. Beliefs and Opinions, "On Worship"
148. Leviticus Rabbah 14.1
149. Niddah 30b
150. Zohar 3:43a-b
151. Ein Yaakov
152. Anchor Bible Leviticus 1-16, pp. 816-23
153. Leviticus Rabbah 16.6
154. Guide III,47
155. Leviticus Rabbah 16.3
156. Zohar 3:52b
157. Book of Legends, 459:532
158. Zohar III, 63a-63b, Raya Mehemna, (Tishby)
159. Hesiod, fragment 6, p. 277
160. Hymn To Pan, XIX, ll. 1-20
161. Leviticus Rabbah 23.9
162. Tanna Debe Eliyyahu, ER p. 75
163. Zohar 3:76b-3:77a
164. Midrash on Psalms 15
165. Midrash on Psalms 146
166. Ecclesiastes Rabbah 9.10
167. Zohar 3:83b-3:84b
168. Guide to Serving God, Chapter 12
169. Leviticus Rabbah 24.5
170. Tanna Debe Eliyyahu, ER p. 19

171. Pesikta Rabbati, Piska 21 and 22
172. Guide III,47
173. Kuzari, 3.48-49 (Korobkin)
174. Guide I,55
175. Zohar 3:87b-3:88a
176. Numbers Rabbah 25.17
177. Zohar 3:85a-b
178. Pirkei de Rabbi Eliezer 51
179. Genesis Rabbah 24.7
180. Midrash on Psalms 12
181. Pirkei de Rabbi Eliezer 48
182. Shelomith: Leviticus Rabbah 32.4; 32.3
183. Midrash Tanḥuma, Shemot; Exodus Rabbah 1:28
184. Zohar 3:106a
185. Leviticus Rabbah 32.3
186. Pesikta Rabbati, 23/24.2
187. Honor parents: Mekhilta de-Rabbi Ishmael, Baḥodesh 8; Nezikin 5
188. Die the death: Mekhilta de-Rabbi Shimon bar Yoḥai 62.3.4; 62.1.2-6
189. Leviticus Rabbah 28.1
190. Pesikta de-Rab Kahana 22.5a
191. Song of Songs Rabbah 2.13
192. Rashi, Leviticus
193. Pesikta Rabbati, 39:1-2
194. Rashi, Leviticus
195. Zohar II, 183a, (Tishby)
196. Money and speech: Book of Legends, 657:186; 661:210-11
197. Mekhilta de-Rabbi Simeon bar Yoḥai, 53.2
198. Mekhilta de-Rabbi Ishmael, Baḥodesh 3
199. Tanna Debe Eliyyahu, ER pp. 95-96
200. Curses into blessings, read and do: Leviticus Rabbah 35.1; 35.6-8
201. Book of Beliefs and Opinions, pp. 327-330
202. Tanna Debe Eliyyahu, ER pp. 95-96
203. Ein Yakov
204. Kuzari, 1:104-109.4 (Korobkin)
205. Pesikta Rabbati, Piska 31.3 and 33.12
206. Leviticus Rabbah 37.2

207. Midrash Tanḥuma, Bechukosai

Numbers

208. Giving and counting: Numbers Rabbah 1.7, 2.11
209. The Art of War, 5.1
210. Book of Legends, 88:82
211. Numbers Rabbah 1.3, 1.6
212. Guide to Serving God, Chapter XII, p. 475
213. Legends of the Jews
214. after *Zohar* III, 124a (Tishby, with variations)
215. Yemenite Midrash, 7.6
216. BT Sotah 3a; Numbers Rabbah 9.12
217. Guide III,46
218. Leviticus Rabbah 9.9
219. Mekhilta de-Rabbi Simeon bar Yoḥai, Nezikin
220. in Maḥazeh Avraham
221. Present at Sinai
222. Midrash Tanḥuma, Be-haalotekha
223. Rashi
224. Numbers Rabbah 15.25
225. BT Sanhedrin 17a
226. Ecclesiastes Rabbah 11.11
227. Numbers Rabbah 15.19
228. Kuzari, pp. 212-215, 101-105
229. Zohar 3:152a
230. Kuzari
231. Guide I; II,45
232. Pesikta Rabbati, Piska 29/30A.5/ Pesikta de-Rab Kahana, Piska 16.4
233. Book of Legends, 728:61
234. Ecclesiastes Rabbah 1.13
235. Zohar 3:159a-b
236. Tanna Debe Eliyyahu, ER pp. 144-45
237. Seder Olam
238. Zohar 3:157a
239. Grasshoppers: Ein Yaakov
240. ANET, 476-77

241. Israel weeping: Numbers Rabbah 16.20, 16.25
242. Tanna Debe Eliyyahu, ER p. 144
243. Pseudo-Philo, OT Pseudepigrapha vol 2, pp. 322-23
244. Numbers Rabbah 18.16-17; 18.13
245. Midrash on Psalms 45
246. Midrash on Psalms 46
247. Numbers Rabbah 18.20
248. BT Sanhedrin 110a
249. Legends of the Jews, v 3, pp. 52-54
250. Zohar V (Soncino) Hukkath 181a-183b
251. Book of Legends 74:70/ 483:130
252. Numbers Rabbah 19.25-26
253. Yalkut, Ḥukkat, §763, found in Book of Legends
254. Survival of the Pagan Gods
255. Midrash on Psalms 24/ Leviticus Rabbah 22.4
256. Guide III,51
257. BT, Baba Bathra, 17a
258. Numbers Rabbah 20.2-9
259. Zohar 206b-208b; 212a-b; 193b-194a
260. Numbers Rabbah 20.15
261. BT Sanhedrin 106a; PT Sanhedrin 10:2, 28d
262. BT Baba Bathra 16a
263. Zohar 184b-185a
264. Pesikta Rabbati, Piska 16.7
265. Zohar I, 229b; III, 256b (Tishby)
266. Guide to Serving God, Chapter VI, pp. 89-91
267. Zohar V (Soncino) Pinḥas 213a-214b
268. Pirke de Rabbi Eliezer 47
269. Exodus Rabbah 43.4
270. Book of Legends, 760:9
271. Midrash on Psalms 79
272. Mekhilta de-Rabbi Ishmael, Pisha, Ch XIV
273. Jewish Magic and Superstition
274. *New Science*, Book II: Poetic Wisdom, Sec 1., Ch. 1
275. Numbers Rabbah 23.1
276. Guide III,50

Deuteronomy

277. Book of Legends, 99:123
278. Blake, Marriage of Heaven and Hell, A memorable Fancy
279. BT Yoma
280. Midrash HaGadol
281. Guide III,9; II,33
282. Midrash HaGadol
283. Rabbenu Baḥya
284. Pirke de Rabbi Eliezer 41
285. Mekhilta de-Rabbi Ishmael, BaHodesh, ch IX
286. Zohar Ḥadash, Exodus 41b
287. Zohar III, 224a-225a (Tishby)
288. Rabbi Yiẓhak of Gur in Siaḥ Sarfei Kodesh
289. Kuzari, pp. 111-112
290. BT Niddah 16b
291. Deuteronomy Rabbah 3.11
292. Book of Legends, 4:14
293. Midrash on Psalms 17
294. Zohar III, 56a-b; 8a (Tishby)
295. Kuzari, pp. 172-3
296. Hedge around the Torah, BT Pirkei Avot, 1:1; Guide III,41
297. Deuteronomy Rabbah 4.1
298. Genesis Rabbah 56.10
299. Tanna Debe Eliyyahu, ER p.19
300. Book of Legends, 79-80:36
301. Midrash on Psalms 25
302. Guide I,38
303. Guide III,35
304. Sifre Deuteronomy, 186-87
305. Pesikta de-Rab Kahana 26.2
306. Midrash on Psalms 17
307. BT Sanhedrin 32b
308. Zohar Ḥadash, Va-yaar, 26 b (Tishby)
309. Pirkei de Rabbi Eliezer 44
310. Midrash on Psalms 9
311. Midrash on Psalms 137
312. Pesikta de-Rab Kahana, Piska 3.6, 3e

313. Book of Legends, 461:543
314. Midrash on Psalms 91
315. trans. Everett Fox
316. Exodus Rabbah 5.9
317. Zohar Ḥadash, Ki Tavo, 59c-60a (Tishby)
318. "53" in Tishby
319. Book of Legends, 403:10; 482:122
320. Kuzari, p. 155
321. Rashi, Deuteronomy
322. Pirke de Rabbi Eliezer 15
323. Beliefs and Opinions, cf. Deuteronomy 29:29
324. Seder Olam
325. BT Hagiga 3
326. Death and Moses: Deuteronomy Rabbah 9.1, 9.9, 9.6-8
327. Guide III,51; I,24
328. BT Baba Bathra 15a
329. PT Horayot 3:5, 48c (found in Book of Legends)
330. Yemenite Midrash 13.5
331. Ecclesiastes Rabbah 1.1, 3.16
332. Midrash on Psalms 90
333. Moses' death: Deuteronomy Rabbah 11.10, 11.5
334. Exodus Rabbah 21.3
335. Midrash Tanḥuma, Ha-azinu
336. Genesis Rabbah 22:2
337. Zohar 3:287a-b
338. Midrash on Psalms 104